A Place Of Significance

Edited by

Heather Killingray

First published in Great Britain in 1998 by
POETRY NOW
1-2 Wainman Road, Woodston,
Peterborough, PE2 7BU
Telephone (01733) 230746
Fax (01733) 230751

All Rights Reserved

Copyright Contributors 1998

HB ISBN 1 86188 666 7
SB ISBN 1 86188 661 6

Foreword

Although we are a nation of poetry writers we are accused of not reading poetry and not buying poetry books: after many years of listening to the incessant gripes of poetry publishers, I can only assume that the books they publish, in general, are books that most people do not want to read.

Poetry should not be obscure, introverted, and as cryptic as a crossword puzzle: it is the poet's duty to reach out and embrace the world.

The world owes the poet nothing and we should not be expected to dig and delve into a rambling discourse searching for some inner meaning.

The reason we write poetry (and almost all of us do) is because we want to communicate: an ideal; an idea; or a specific feeling. Poetry is as essential in communication, as a letter; a radio; a telephone, and the main criteria for selecting the poems in this anthology is very simple: they communicate.

How many of you have a special place, a place where you can just be yourself? Ask a poet that question and you get an abundance of answers from 'Grandma's kitchen' to 'Skegness'. Most people find peace and inspiration in these special places and with it a sense of belonging.

What better way to start your thoughts rolling by being introduced to these places in the words of the poets themselves.

'A Place Of Significance' is an apt title for this anthology. Read from cover to cover you will understand why the poets write about that place and who knows, you may even join them.

CONTENTS

The Silkstead Road	Marion Primrose	1
My Place	Joyce Goldie	2
Swedish Winter	Rex Baker	3
UN Stratford Branch	Peter Wykes	4
All Change In Suburbia	Valerie Hockaday	5
Woolacombe	Les Hinton	6
Autumn At Icklesham	Joan Howes	7
Under Water	Kenneth Mood	8
The Flowers Of Moorcroft Wood Wednesbury Wotansburg	David Thompson	9
Voices In The Attic	Jean Marsden	10
Lord Nelson	June Fricker	11
That Quiet Place	Peter Vaughan Williams	12
Market Day In My Home Town	Jan Caswell	13
A Place On The Map	Geoffrey Mason	14
Return To Dante's Tomb	Edgar Wyatt Stephens	15
Maryland In The Fall	Betty Curnow	16
On A Winter's Day	Christine Noden	17
Avenue In Eden	Sylvia Brice	18
An Afternoon At Bridlington	Anne Mullender	19
My Childhood	B Hibbert	20
Forest Gate Cemetery	Margaret Gosley	21
Senses Of A Mother	Karen Moon	22
Charlotte, Emily And Anne	Geoffrey Price	23
A Lovely Place	Joan Scher	24
The Postcard	Barbara Henry	25
The Tree	Jeanne Brown	26
Beauty And Us	Joyce Barry	27
Bryce Canyon	Margaret C Rae	28
Mist	Robert W Lockett	29
The Rolling Hills Of Ashton's Green	Peter Waring	30
To Dream	Beryl Sylvia Rusmanis	31
Spirit Source Says	Catherine Roberts	32
Coming Home	Doreen Kerley	33

October Half-Term		
At Coniston	Mandy Archer	34
The Gardens Of Remembrance	Susan Gray	35
Talking of Athens . . .	David Daymond	36
Old Spain	Philippa Sampson	37
The Bottom Of The Garden	Barbara M Brown	38
Swing Gardens	Debra Ingram	39
On The Edge	Trudi Carroll	40
We Could Have Scored Seven	Terri Grech	41
The Secret Place	Anne Murray	42
Whitsuntide Walk	Joan Milner	43
Noon At The Lakeside	Keith Taylor	44
My Toe	Janet Dickson	45
Post Office	Lynn Marsden	46
Joy	J Harrington	47
November Dawns	Elizabeth Coop	48
East Anglia	M I Maggs	49
Essence Of All Our Yesterdays	J D Ashton	50
Seachange	Bill Murphy	51
Brave Oak	K Scarfe	52
The Snapshot	John Bryant	53
The Cemetery	Joanne Gough	54
By No Means Homeless	Rosemary Wells	55
The Abbey	Sheila Durbin	56
Wreck Diving	Anthony le Feuvre	57
Down And Out	Jill M Ronald	58
Our Church	Dorothy Lloyd	59
Claypit Wood	Alison Vernon	60
Along The River Neb	Maisie Sell	61
Crab Cottage. Present And Past	Rosemary Y Vendell	62
Level With Earth	Chris Moat	63
A Remembered Place	L Simcock-Daisy	64
Cold	K Axon	65
Moonlit Meadow	Jorjana Franklin	66
Starry Sky	F J Carradus	67
A Windy Day On The		
Norfolk Broads	J S Maidwell	68
Unexpected	Myasser Ashraf	69

The Garden	Anand Deshpande	70
Untitled	Helen Harlow	71
Even Wolves Can Dream	Joan Galpin	72
Night Storm	Henry J Green	73
Dorset Gap	Kersty Strong	74
The Circle Of Time	E Walker	75
The Little Things	P D Taylor	76
A Sanctuary True	Katrina M Greenhalf	77
Moors In Winter	Elaine Goodman	78
East Berlin	Hazel Browne	79
Bluebells	J M Rowe	80
South Devon	E Eveleigh	81
Landscape	Mary Hughes	82
A Tribute To Those Who Died	M Dury	83
Our Dear River Ver	Owen Edwards	84
Memories	Gwen Walsh	86
Bird Brain Feather Wait	Bryan William Green	87
The Stream	Jan Pollard	88
The Visitor	Ruth Suffolk	89
The Window	Susan Roberts	90
A Bridge At Dusk	Mary Quinlan	91
When I Remember	George B Burns	92
Oban's Bay	Katrina Holland	93
Daydreams	H Livesey	94
Kirk Fell	Michael James Fuller	95
Skeggy	Tony Bowers	96
Isle Of Eigg 1984	Edwina Vardey	97
When The Sun Crosses The Celestial Equator	Judith Anne Carmichael	98
Culloden Memorial	John Clarke	99
Sunset In The Trees	Sarah Hardy	100
Skylines	Beryl Stockman	101
Belfast	Francis McFaul	102
Busy Café	Marjorie Cowan	103
Brighton Carousel	Chris Malcomson	104
Triumph Of The Spirit	Mair H Thomas	105
Winter's Memory	Joyce Barton	106
Untitled	Jay Hendricks	107

Title	Author	Page
This Place Is . . . ?	Bill Hogg	108
The Hospital	Lesley Dearman	109
Glimpses Of India	Shirley Johnson	110
Show Birds	Brian O'Brien	111
Morning Walk In Kusadasi - Turkey	Heather Walker	112
Cornish Dream	Amy Oldham	113
Summer Garden	Jean Roughton	114
The Wind That Shakes The Barley	Michael Thorpe	115
Untitled	James Slater	116
Upon The Hills	Steven J Smith	117
Grandmother's Kitchen	Poppy Meredith	118
Mablethorpe's Challenge To My Refusal To Gamble	Gillian Fisher	119
Rain At Weirwood Reservoir	Margaret Gibian	120
Vienna	Joan Letts	121
Spectres	Claire Partridge	122
The Harbour	Sarah Lightbody	123
My Country Lane	Elaine Beresford	124
My Retreat	Patricia A Atkin	125
A Sad Farewell	Rosamund Hudson	126
The Monument	K D Thomas	127
Summer In Oklahoma	Jane Upchurch	128
The Old Church	Isobel M Maclarnon	129
The Track	Jacquie L Smith	130
A Winter Cold	Suzan Gumush	131
The Orchard	Helen Lansdown	132
My Heavenly Garden	Joan Marian Jones	133
In Harpford Woods	Peter Chaney	134
Untitled	Malcolm Bell	135
The Empty House	P R Mason	136
Lament For The Passing Of The Front Garden	Maureen A Jones	137
A Glen In Antrim	Julian Ronay	138
Mexico	Kiran Shah	139
In This Place	Anne Byron	140
Florence	Barbara Fosh	141

Ty Mawr	Bill Johnson	142
Springtime In The Country	Neil McClafferty	144
In The Middle Of The Night	Rosetta Stone	145
The Garden	Bob Wydell	146
The Cottage In Wales	Sally M McNab	147
The Oak Tree	Olive Bedford	148
Pharmacy Warfare	Sara Russell, Golden Eagles	149
As I Sit Here (Belgium 1986)	Harry H Rolfe	150
Holiday Cottage	Susan Goldsmith	152
As I Look Up	Ian Fowler	153
Sunday School	Maisie Cottingham	154
Memories	Margaret D'Sa	155
My Haven	Christina Crowe	156
Port Isaac North Cornwall	Colin Farmer	157

THE SILKSTEAD ROAD

Tramping Yew Hill, thick bluebelled Silkstead Road,
I thought: did monks eye peacock butterflies?
Did they appreciate what nature showed -
stitchwort, ground ivy, wood anemones?
We took equivocal arrowheads, prised
from the chalk path. I wanted to believe
each blue white flint was pottery disguised;
ancient shards. I so desired to receive
visions of men canopied under trees,
cathedral vaulted, dim tunnelled walkway.
I thought we heard thin voices on the breeze,
chanting plainsong. Perhaps it was the day,
so clear, that put such notions in my head,
its wildflower profusion resurrection
in itself. Perhaps those we thought long dead
haunt such paths, bringing their benediction.

Marion Primrose

My Place

Cream washed walls surround me
As in a warm embrace,
Rose coloured beams from the window
Weave stained-glass forms on my face.

Silence, except for the sound of the sea
Candle flames straight in the absence of breeze
Cross on the altar draws my eyes
As I quietly sink to my knees.

Dust motes dance in my breathing
Gulls in the harbour cry.
The tiny church at the foot of the hill
Is my place, and there's good reason why.

It's where I've been 'home' since I moved here
Where communities meet and blend
Where we all serve each other because of our Lord
Where, in friendship, our troubles can mend.

Joyce Goldie

SWEDISH WINTER

So still in the silent whiteness of snow
Where even time's supremacy expires
The earth rests limpid in a frosty glow
That quenches man's conceit and his desires.

Dark Smorland's forests, Hair-yedalen's fells
Or graceful Skorney's undulating plains
All wear the same bright livery that tells
Of winter's rapture and its hidden pains.

Now through the spindly lattices of birch
A milky moonlight threads its pallid beams
Whilst in the sombre graveyard of a church
Lie frozen human sorrows, loves and dreams.

A world which bears no hues nor makes a sound
Declares its brief eternity of peace,
The beauty of an instant so profound
That neither art nor willing can increase.

Though just as deep beneath an icy pall
Lie other lands in winter's cool embrace,
No vision of its splendour will enthral
So much as Sweden's days and nights and space.

Rex Baker

UN STRATFORD BRANCH

Old cottage,
Timbers steeped in history,
Mecca for students,
Literature lovers
And plain slight seers.

I wander in silence,
Wondering at Tudor relics,
Wondering that written words
Could perpetuate a man's fame
For almost four centuries.

Yanks are there in force,
Forgetting separation by common language
Or perhaps seeking something
Deeper than words alone,
They send twanging tone
To cut the air
Of musty rooms.

I hear guttural accents
Of strapping young Germans
Dissecting the moment:
More musical French,
And other tongues I cannot place.

Outside a group of
Camera-hung Japanese
Twitter like be-spectacled sparrows.

People from around the globe,
Drawn to the Bard's birthplace,
Forming Stratford's own branch
Of the United Nations.

Peter Wykes

ALL CHANGE IN SUBURBIA

Lace curtains flap their filigree,
Drowsy, sunny doorways sport striped canvas covers,
Identikit houses enclose a secret family about their private business.
Pin-suited fathers descend the cavernous tube-train,
Emerging promptly at six each evening,
Mysterious doings in the city.
An air of gentle respectability pervades,
Tea is taken on the lawn, a tinkle of silver conversation,
'Life's so vulgar, please don't mention money!'

Side-step the indigenous, another wave moves in:
Strange sounding lengthy surnames,
Black-eyed grannies sit and sun on porches,
Exotic vegetables labelled in hieroglyphs,
Money pinned on babies, plates smashed at weddings,
The whirr of sewing machines on summer evenings
Stitch up a couture venture.
Intimations of enterprise and chinking coins
Puncture this capital corner,
Where the fluttering, pristine nets
Proclaim a tidy profit.

Valerie Hockaday

WOOLACOMBE

Rolling surf, crashing waves
   pour onto pure white sand.
With slate like rugged rocks
   to make a picture grand.

Its many changing faces
   skies of blue or grey.
Seas of an emerald green
   and a white soft spray.

Many craggy clifftop walks
   that go for miles and miles.
Lush green valleys, grassy slopes
   the scenery it just beguiles.

Blue flags are always flying
   to show the sea is clean.
A place that we call Woolacombe
   the place that is supreme.

Les Hinton

AUTUMN AT ICKLESHAM

Sussex lay ripe as a pippin
In the warm palm of an ember afternoon.
Orchards stood still and spent
Among the windfalls
Of their lustrous yield.
A rising sweep of grassland
Curved to the windmill's base,
The surge of blades lapping
White palings with dancing stalks.
A rustic stile wore a shimmering dragonfly
Pinned for a lazuli moment
To its topmost bar.
Dark riches of autumn fruit
Gleamed through tremulous leaves,
Adorning the moment with glad gifts
Before the first frosts blew
Their glittering stealth
Along shining leaf-rims.
Touching hands and senses
With chill presage.
A shudder of portent
Belying the transient gold.
Needling among unspoken admissions
Of sharp need.
The metallic chime
Of unaccompanied footsteps.

Joan Howes

UNDER WATER

Fish danced beside the rocks,
Coral filled my eyes.
Then I climbed out the sea
To see your smile,
The rainbow behind your head
Reminded me of angel fish going
Into a Caribbean cave.

Kenneth Mood

THE FLOWERS OF MOORCROFT WOOD
WEDNESBURY WOTANSBURG

Wistful wisps of mist dancing in beams of light,
Were following an ancient rite offering, sweet,
Soporific, gifts, scents of last year's leafy souls,
To singing birds in blossoming trees, awakened
By the warming rays of Moorcroft where once
A forest grew.

The spirit of this wood takes hold, it offers
Something long denied, quenching of some hidden
Thirst, for all, who can; 'Drink Deeply', along
A lake witch-hazels grow, as do rags in
Plastic bags. Deeds done by people who couldn't
Sense their souls. In a grasping world they appear
To have lost their own. No room for mere enchantment
In a magic place. In the modern world of haste
The likes of that have been replaced.

A tarmac path leads to towering pines. In this
Court in autumn's past. Lawyers' wigs judged all
Who passed. Thinning out trees give way to a boggy
Place of sedge, treading on paper plates you come
Upon a parking place. Here you read a sign which
Says *'No Guns'*.

But young men lusting just to kill, shot a goose
One day, whilst peacefully swimming on the lake
A pellet took her life. Distraught a gander swims
Alone. *'Fear, famine, fire and flood'* the flowers
Of Moorcroft may mourn for us as a forest grows.

David Thompson

VOICES IN THE ATTIC

One day, going up there,
I heard the three of you
Quite plainly, in the musty air.
Your forgotten clothes
In that old trunk,
Revived memories
That long ago had shrunk
To nothing, and almost slunk
Beyond repair.

At the table, back to the wall,
There was the clamour
For the 'alone' place
Opposite the other two,
Parents presiding at each end
And umpiring it all.

Then there was the stress
Over that party dress,
And there the high chair,
The dropside cot,
Abandoned by the stair.
No thought then
Of grandchildren,
Just the relish of more space
About the place.
Few toys survived
Spring cleaning exercise,
Unless you count
A Davy Crocket hat,
And the grimy grain
Of an old cricket bat.

Jean Marsden

LORD NELSON

He was our national hero,
Lord Nelson, was his name,
'The Battle of Trafalgar',
Not his only claim to fame,
A man full of compassion,
For the sailors, in his charge,
A big, big man, in every way,
Though his stature, wasn't large,
His ship was called, 'The Victory',
Magnificent, and proud,
For he brought out, the best in men,
They sang his praise out loud,
'The Battle of Trafalgar',
Was where our hero fell,
The date was eighteen hundred and five,
We know our history well,
He lay there wounded on the deck,
His face all racked with pain,
His sailors carried him below,
Our great, 'Sea Lord' was slain,
His faithful 'Hardy' by his side,
As the battle raged on high,
It was his final victory,
It was his place to die,
He stands now in 'Trafalgar Square',
To all, a thing of beauty,
A tribute to a great, great man,
Thank God, he did his duty . . .

June Fricker

THAT QUIET PLACE

Deep inside the space between the tall forest trees is that place,
For some reason the spectrums in your hair shone strong and
Then lit up your eyes within your lovely face amidst quiet grass.
The haphazard pace of the ladybird within your fingers curling,
While the dragonflies skimmed brook trail throughout songbird sound.
These days that place is no longer for with you gone quiet is re-paced
By my grief stricken rage. In that quiet place nobody hears me scream,
While missing you each single day, along that gladed stream.

Peter Vaughan Williams

MARKET DAY IN MY HOME TOWN

An exodus of farming folk
From hilltop fresh and valley smoke.
Making their way, as best they can
By horse-drawn cart or gypsy van.
Best salted bacon piled up high
With rows of crusty home-made pie.
Drums of butter and jugs of cream,
Home-made broth in cauldrons steam.
Red-faced old ladies, dressed in black
Selling earth apples from a sack.
Barrels of apples red and green
Adding to the colourful scene.
Wicker baskets overflow with eggs.
Rainbow gypsies selling pegs.
Dogs start barking, as cockerel crows.
Doomed fatted calves in silent rows.
Young lovers strolling side by side.
Best friends sharing a donkey ride.
Pick-pockets mingle where rich men stand
Watching the conjurers slight of hand.
Squealing piglets slip from their pen
Chased by several shrewd-eyed men.
Drunken brawls in back streets begin.
Eyes are blackened, knuckles skin.
Over-ripe apples roll down the street,
Crushed by many pounding feet.
Working horses pull carts along
The day for them is much too long.
Stalls dismantled, as sun goes down.
Market day's over, in my home town.

Jan Caswell

A Place On The Map

Your memory keeps revisiting the house
with grey pebble-dash, a brown front door,
a hopscotch pavement outside the gate

and a white bay-window
where a child is practising
your signature with a new fountain-pen.

It visits the library across the rec,
smells the polish and watches the transaction
of your tickets exchanged for books,

and uphill there's a yellow-brick church
crowded and choired for evensong
where you stare love and get stared back.

>   Slide the flat stone to land on 12,
>   hop to 11, pick it up,
>   turn round and hop back to square 1.

You don't, you don't, and then one day
you do go back, only to see
how others will remember where they lived -

young faces at the window of a house
whose face you hardly recognised.
Their parents don't know unlocked doors

and shops behind just glass at night,
workdays with full buses passing queues.
Only the road names haven't changed

where children walk to school
reading the work of war poets
sprayed on walls by living hands.

Geoffrey Mason

RETURN TO DANTE'S TOMB

Transformed as the photos, tints have faded
Into memories imprinted black and white;
The leaning tower's grandeur's now been traded,

Abrogated for Ravenna's niche of light -
Shaded, dusted, bricked barricaded passage
Iron barred, resisting monstrous howling night.

In breathless hush the grave imparts its message
Before tumult's silent stifling breathless pause,
Abandoned hopes, abandoned faiths, dread presage,

Its chill effect, abandoned God the cause.
Even now, in watch, the Giver's angel's face
Each mourner dwindling June's pale light still draws

In breathless love, unto this breathless place,
To love, as knowing half of paradise; yet,
Not to be loved as inferno's full embrace.

Inferno's fires, refiner's fires beget
To keep live in time what timely love brings soon
And keep it spring in June's warm sweetness wet.

Oh, winter blasts are not death's sombre tune.
That's the dusty teardrops falling, ending June.

Edgar Wyatt Stephens

MARYLAND IN THE FALL

The glorious trees spread all around as far as the eye can see
Thickly clothed in orange, yellow, red and mulberry
Through this autumn wonderland the quiet road winds down
Picturesquely strewn with leaves by gentle breezes blown
Sunlight filters through the branches, warming with its rays
Casting out the shadows from the darkened woodland ways
Overhead a flock of geese on leisured wing go by
Their noisy clamouring breaking the stillness of the sky
Countless squirrels dart about this quiet countryside
Always busy in their search for food and nuts to hide
Rushing rivers run their course in the journey to the sea
Whilst in the distance mountains reign in quiet majesty
A sense of peace pervades here mid verdant land and sky
A spiritual refreshment and I'm so glad that I
Was privileged to be a part and see these sights first hand
And never will forget that special time in Maryland.

Betty Curnow

On A Winter's Day

On a winter's day
I walked into a cafe
Warmth of the room felt so inviting
The aroma of the coffee was enticing

The noisy coffee machines were on
I had to speak up quite loud
To gain the assistant's attention
She asked me what I would like
A cup of coffee would be so nice
And a bun made of sugar and spice

The people were talking quite loud to hear
Themselves speak as I went to my seat
The coffee tasted so good
And the bun was so delicious too
It warmed me up quite through

The coffee machines were so noisy
I had a headache coming on
So I went out into the snow
Found that my headache had gone

Christine Noden

AVENUE IN EDEN

We left the beach and wandered through
The gates of heaven, so it seemed;
An avenue of trees and flowers,
An eden such as we had dreamed.

The stately homes stood either side
With each one different to the eye;
Their hedges barring trespassers
And trees that grew up to the sky.

The road was smooth and wide and long,
A pathway through a promised land;
The tranquil air was undisturbed
And peace and joy walked hand in hand.

Although the day was burning hot
There was a coolness in the lane;
The trees bent down to shade our heads,
The silence echoed through our brain.

We stopped and sat upon the grass
So green from rains that came before;
To whisper seemed to be a sin
As nature opened up her door.

This is indeed a sceptred isle,
Sublime in all its majesty;
But even so this avenue
Was eden just for you and me.

Sylvia Brice

AN AFTERNOON AT BRIDLINGTON

The afternoon sea is calm today
Gently the tide comes in
Two ladies stand at the water's edge
The waves caress their feet.

Whilst on the golden beach
A yellow kite flies high
Held by a little fair-haired boy
Oblivious to the heat.

Nearby the donkeys wait.
Two little girls come running
'Please may we have a ride?' they ask
And pay their seventy p.

The donkeys meander up the beach
Mother takes some photos
All too soon the ride is done
'Can we have something to eat?'

Mother hands the picnic round
The little girls say 'Thank you'
The fair-haired boy says to his Mum
'I want ice-cream to eat!'

Anne Mullender

MY CHILDHOOD

Stockport is the place I love
It's where I started out.
Scrimped and scraped I did
Still ended up with nowt.

Played in the cobbled streets
With me marbles and me hoop.
Friends thought me barmy
So I'd go and loop the loop.

I played in me go-cart
With me brother Pete.
Crashed it round a lamppost
In the summer heat.

I'd go off biking in the sun
Not a care in me head.
Take a butty and some fizzy pop
But be back in time for bed.

I'd play hopscotch and tag
Then skating up the street.
Then knock on all the doors
So all me friends could meet.

Mine was a happy childhood
Plenty to be done.
And with me parents being around
They made it so much fun.

I did enjoy me childhood
With so much to remember.
Fun, games and laughter
From January to December.

B Hibbert

FOREST GATE CEMETERY

On a day like today the angels in the cemetery
Do not look heavenwards, instead
They huddle together, a little bedraggled,
Wings drooping, hanging their heads.

Their angel hands are clasped in prayer
Whilst here and there, on soft ground,
Wrought iron gates to Paradise tilt and rust
Ashes to ashes, dust to dust.

Beside and beneath, the virgin girls in stony gowns
Cling to their crosses whilst the ivy binds
Them to the cold, wet ground
And all around the broken columns of the young men stand
Granite cold, resisting embrace,
Silent and stunned against the grey sky.

There are Bibles whose pages will not turn
As lichen blurs the sentiments written in stone
And the draped urn looks empty
Cold ashes with the soul long gone.

Margaret Gosley

SENSES OF A MOTHER

So still, so warm, so light, so sweet,
So small, so fragile tiny hands and feet,
The smell of creams and talc lingers,
As if it could be touched by fingers.
A warm glow seems all around,
As if something magical has been found.
A soft murmur fills the air,
Another follows without a care.
I tread softly as to make no sound,
Just as snow would cover ground,
A movement, I stand quite still,
Words can't catch how I feel,
A tingling all over as I stand and stare,
In his cot, my baby son,
So small, so fair,
A sense of love,
A bond so deep,
A feeling that mother and son
Will always keep.

Karen Moon

CHARLOTTE, EMILY AND ANNE

There's a darkness in the hallway
A cold, cold silence hangs about
Now that the final candle
Has flickered and died out.

The wind without the four walls
Turns its whisper to a weep
But neither wind nor rain can enter
Where all the sisters sleep.

Out across the moorlands
The winter's packed and gone
And springtime reigns majestic
As the first new lambs are born.

But the sisters now see nothing
There is a darkness in their eyes
Imprisoned thus forever
Nor door nor window to the skies.

Time has passed and proven
Each one equal to any man
Though the candles all burned out a long time ago
For Charlotte, Emily and Anne.

Geoffrey Price

A Lovely Place

The river Esk, flows gently underneath the brig,
The golden sun, sends glory, up on yonder rig.
I see a water vole, paddling quickly by,
A slow worm, slithering, and then a butterfly
Sampling honeysuckle, heavy fragrance sweet,
A cheeky little sparrow comes hopping near my feet.

He knows there will be crumbs to peck,
As I picnic quietly here,
Oh what a thrill, a kingfisher
Has flashed across the weir.

If we can find some time to spare,
There's such beauty we can see,
This is a lovely place today,
With wonders, here for me.

Joan Scher

THE POSTCARD

Wish you were here - the postcard says,
But how can I describe,
The lift of my heart
And the sheer delight,
At the view before my eyes.

Weather lovely - the postcard says,
But I can't really say,
How the sun spreads a warmth
That touches my soul,
As the scent of flowers fills the air.

Scenery wonderful - the postcard says,
But I cannot put across,
The splendour of mountains
Reflected below,
In lakes of mirrored glass.

But at least you will know
From my postcard,
That I have thought of you,
As I relax on my holiday,
Then return, refreshed and renewed.

Barbara Henry

THE TREE

Standing, silently proud against the wild sky
This stalwart of England.
A giant with voiceless secrets.
Unuttered stories held in monumental empty arms.
Standing proud against a blue/grey sky,
Holding new life gently.
Mute. Whispering but speechless.
Arms twisted, entwined,
Beckoning to all.

Thousands of years he has stood,
Knowing all, telling nothing,
Whispering.
Passing on his stories to the wind.
The ground trembles at its utterances
Scattering life, only to shoot up at another place.

Standing proud against an azure sky
Guarding its secrets boldly.
Once tamed, now wild like the garden.
Look closely, how many have carved their names?
How many have lain, entwined in its roots?
Or resting from the toil of labour?

Thousands of years he has stood,
Knowing all, telling nothing,
Impenetrable.
The ravages of time will decide its fate.
Not fire or axe to yield the final blow.
Time will be *its* destiny.

Jeanne Brown

BEAUTY AND US

Dad had a motorcycle combination
A beauty, he'd proudly say, BSA,
Engine very impressive
Roared, when kicked into action
Can't remember how many horses
Thundering, big, and strong
Pulled us to our destination.

We liked going to Brighton
50 miles there, 50 miles back
An easy run for our beauty
Crawling through Tooting and Croydon
Warming up to Dorking then Crawley
To the new duel carriageway
Throttle open, picking up speed
Pounding along so excitingly
AA Patrolman salutes, coming fast
Whines and z o o ms going past
The deep steady throb of the engine
Humming and tuned, strangely satisfying
As we lick the miles into Brighton town.

Joyce Barry

BRYCE CANYON

Bryce Canyon is a sight to see
It is unbelievable and rare.
The rock shapes are called hoodoos,
I've never seen rocks so bare,
But there are trees growing too,
Don't let me mislead you on that.
The shapes of the hoodoos
Are all different, some thin, some fat.

There was one that looked like the Sphinx.
Cinderella's castle is in there too,
And the ugly sisters and a dog,
With minarets and spires in a queue.

The view is spectacularly fine,
It just goes on and seems to soar.
It does seem like on a clear day
You can see for ever more.

We admire what mankind has made,
With his many inventions so great,
But when we see such wonders
Mother Nature can create,
Man's home-made creations dim
And fade like a will o' the wisp,
Before natural phenomenons like this,
So clear, so deep, so crisp.

Margaret C Rae

MIST

There is something about the mist I like,
The way it hovers above the grass,
Obscures the trees from bole to leaf,
And blankets out the sky confusing light.

I have often seen mornings like these,
They bring with them a sense
Of beginning, the fresh start
Of a new day's dawning.

Such mornings as these are lovely to perceive,
With moisture forming on grass and leaf,
And a stillness that is deep,
Yet always awake, that never sleeps.

We sleep and do not see the mist
Form silently around us, quietly it comes,
Slowly yet determined and in darkness
To start the day anew.

Such mornings as these are innocent of dreams,
For there are no secrets here,
No artificial world of means, no dross,
No pain, no suffering, no loss.

At the earth's first dawn, a mist
Went up and watered all the land,
And there was no thirst, no hunger,
No fear, no curse, on that first glorious morn.

Robert W Lockett

THE ROLLING HILLS OF ASHTON'S GREEN

Beneath the rolling hills of Ashton's Green
Lie the playgrounds of my childhood dreams
Where as a child I roamed so happily
To play-out my youthful fantasies

Those gentle slopes where towering slag-heaps then
With sheets of water lapping at the rim
Red rocks of shale stood stark in silhouette
Cast grotesque shadows down the gully beds

Wild indians with war-cries in their throats
Rushed headlong down the steep red dusty slopes
To join in fierce combat hand-to-hand
With Custer's fateful blue clad cavalry band

That towering rock of shale was Everest
Where Hunt and party reached that elusive crest
Brave conquerors of that mean edifice
To lay its myths and mysteries to rest

From the beach at Normandy we fought our way
In desperate battles through the fields and lanes
Of France and Germany to wrest the yoke
On Nazi tyranny from enslaves throats

So many fantasies we then played out
In joyful glee and youthful happy shout
On that playground of my childhood dreams
Beneath the rolling hills of Ashton's Green

Peter Waring

To Dream

I would like to dream
Of going to places I haven't seen,
To taste exotic fruits of life
And have a gamble with a dice.

Why do my thoughts go astray?
I ask myself this question each day,
Should we be contented with what we have got?
And accept it, as being just our lot.

I don't know the reason why,
But who knows, perhaps one day I'll try
And answer all these questions I ask,
Perhaps it will be quite a simple task.

But still I do like to dream,
Makes me feel I am sailing down a stream
And when I wake up to reality,
To me, the day becomes a speciality.

Beryl Sylvia Rusmanis

SPIRIT SOURCE SAYS

. . . Blustery air beats my hair out of place
As I stand on the sand watching waves as they race
To where I am planted bewitched by their pace
And vitality of life which is hard to replace.

Their strength sends me hope and the courage I need
To fight this tough battle that's tried breaking me.

So now I'm awake
I'm quick and I'm sharp
My legs spring to life
I turn and I dart
Away from the water
Who powered my heart
To the cruelty of mortals
To rip it apart!

. . . How clearly I picture that day years ago
When I was so ready to end all I'd known.
My life, soul and self I realise I owe
To my blue spirit source who told me to *go!*

Catherine Roberts

COMING HOME

From these windows I can see,
the land my parents used to till.
Now fifty or more years have passed,
the sight can thrill me still.

Although I had to move away,
I left a long time past.
I'm back again to work the land
and I am home at last.

Doreen Kerley

OCTOBER HALF-TERM AT CONISTON
(Waiting for Gondola)

And so to watching
wet light fading,
drowning, drizzling afternoon.
Tangible dampness, rounding, clouding,
filters the lake-side trees, diffusing
sinking twilight, softening hills.

Grey, wall-masked roads,
unheadlamp-lighted
webb unseen, worn tourist ways;
wend to the lake assorted walkers;
damp cold trailing, toddler wailing;
striding hardies undismayed.

Nearer the pleasure-steamer narrows
silent water space between;
white cabined, anorak bedecking,
black stack streaming, thrusting prow

follows a worn but less marked passage,
bank to bank and end to ending,
jetty closing, jetty leaving,
tips out its fall-time, half-term cargo
into lakeland's wet half-night.

Mandy Archer

THE GARDENS OF REMEMBRANCE

Let's walk amongst the roses
and smell the scented air,
let's linger by the lilies
and gaze at their beauty so fair.

We'll stop for awhile by the daffodils
so plain and simple they be,
but their golden tones bloom in my heart
and blossoms a memory.

And still we wonder of the pansies
as they cast their magic spell.

Let's walk aside the crocuses
together your hand in mine,
even the simple daisies
around our hearts entwine.

But always we return to the roses
and leave behind the rest,
for beneath their fragrant petals
I laid your soul to rest.

To the world I stand by these roses alone
they simply do not see
but as I walk in these gardens of remembrance
I know you walk with me.

Susan Gray

TALKING OF ATHENS . . .

After walking in Athens,
the noise one remembers
is not the impatient clamour
of congested city traffic,
or the continual hammer
of pneumatic drills, or even
the far more sympathetic
age-old ring of stone-chisels
perpetually chipping away
at white Pentelic building marble,
but the sound, the incessant babble
of people talking.

Up to your high hotel window
it swirls around above clouds of dust
and the crowded hot street's glare,
comes as a loud blare,
then blurred, softer, quieter, pianissimo,
surges as the sea out below
the temple at Cape Sunion -
the sound of Athenians
just arguing, shouting, laughing,
talk-talk-talking as, long ago,
under the Agora's colonnades
this Greek city polity
wrangled the world into shape.

David Daymond

OLD SPAIN

If a superficial tan or a plastic Spanish fan
is all you hope to gain; then take a boring plane

However, if you drive, old Spain will come alive
high roads wind back and fore while golden eagles soar
pine trees in gorges grow, white walls glint far below
a lake comes into sight awash in bright sunlight

Spread over the plain of proverbial rain
many miles of grape vines string out in long lines
pickers back bending, a task never-ending
to make tasty wine from the fruit of the vine

The road now descends round precarious bends
bowling down from the plain to the valley again
through dusty olive groves in undulating rows
and flitting dragonflies enormous in size

From wide open spaces to quaint narrow places
relax with a wine and step back in time
where old men sit dozing and young bloods are posing
hollow hand clapping, flamenco foot tapping

Grey mules and jackasses piled high with dry grasses
straw hats all askew, loppy ears poking through
a church on the hill, the heady Bougainvillea
and a dry river bed on its way to the Med

So if it's sun seeking and plain English speaking
then travel to Spain in a 'miss it all' plane

Philippa Sampson

THE BOTTOM OF THE GARDEN

There is magic at the bottom of the garden,
Black shadows shift and flicker beneath overhanging trees,
It is eerie in the darkness for the night is never silent
There is rustling in the undergrowth and whispering in the breeze

There's a Presence at the bottom of the garden,
I can always feel it when I stand there all alone,
It's not an evil presence, of that I'm almost certain
But I get a little thrilling tingle I must own.

The bottom of the garden is a place of mystery
A secret magic place where I can always be
Quite certain, if I go there at dusk and quietly
That thrilling unknown presence will be waiting there for me.

Barbara M Brown

SWING GARDENS

Someone was cutting their grass
The fresh sweet smell tickled my nostrils
And carried me back along the path of childhood,
To days when I lived in the shadow
Of the towering grey concrete monster,
Our home, nine storeys up in the sky.
The cruel concrete yard was my garden,
Littered with the flowers I picked,
Lyons Maid ice-lolly wrappers,
Smiths crisps packets,
My brand name bouquet,
The park was my retreat,
But - I had to watch out
The park keeper, a praying mantis,
Enforced the *keep off the grass* rule
Like his life depended on it.
Don't pick the flowers,
Stay only on the path
So, obediently I would sit,
On my special bench,
Listening to the whirr of the mower
Drinking in the cut grass smell,
Dreaming of the garden I would have,
When I grew big.
Someone was cutting their grass,
Walking on it, picking the flowers,
Planting more -
Someone was very happy - it was me!

Debra Ingram

ON THE EDGE

Standing on the edge of the murky waters of happenings long ago
I feel the cold dampening mist surround me, as if to say, 'Don't go'
Then, almost invited the empty greyness reaches in and wraps itself
                                                         around my heart,
From this endless, weeping, shapeless form, I don't have the
                                                         strength to depart.
It drags me along from day to day under a heavy dark cloak of
                                                         deepening misery
If only a ray of God's sunshine could reach through the mist and
                                                         comfort me
If only it could shine so bright, so as to cradle and lift me from this
                                                         devil's delight,
Then maybe I shall have courage to live again, and for my life I will
                                                         clearly fight.

Trudi Carroll

WE COULD HAVE SCORED SEVEN

Adults and children alike,
Descend from every angle,
Thronging towards a centre point,
That draws them like a magnet.
The smell of chips hangs in the air,
That is heavy with anticipation and excitement,
The roar gets louder as the ground approaches,
Then rises up to meet the crowd as they enter the stands.
Cigarette smoke mingles with beer and tea fumes,
As the crowd shouts its approval to the entering home-team -
The goalie big and strong who flies through the air like an eagle,
The winger, fleet of foot like an Arabian stallion,
The midfielder broad and stout like an army tank,
And the striker, as agile and cunning as a fox,
Join their team-mates in the salute to the fans.
There is a buzz amongst the crowd as the whistle blows,
Then the action flows from end to end,
Like a communal tennis game.
Suddenly the fox seizes his chance and homes in on the ball,
Shooting it through the air like an arrow,
Straight past the despairing lunge of the 'keeper,
The crowd rise in a united wave of joy,
And grown men hug each other in delight.
All too soon it is over,
And young children are carried home aloft Daddy's broad shoulders,
Men huddle in groups, eating warm pies,
And even though one goal separated both teams,
'We could have scored seven.'

Terri Grech

THE SECRET PLACE

Later, when she had rested, the Earth said:
'Let there be sight, and sound, and taste, and smell,
    and touch, and memory.'

So the man and the woman walked in the forest
where the swift, sure-footed squirrel ran;
then on to a hillside of orchid and tormentil.

Their footsteps cracked a path through the bracken
while buzzards circled high with mewing call.

They paused to drink from the stream; and kiss.

As the bee chose its flower,
The man recognised the scent of thyme.

They stroked the mossy bark of ancient oak,
fingered the bristle of lichen on stone.

Then they rested and remembered and shared unspoken thoughts.

'But let all these be secret things, so that
the orchid is unaware of its colour, the waterfall deaf to its own roar;
Nor the man nor the woman understand their love
nor know the line of the path they follow.'

Anne Murray

WHITSUNTIDE WALK

Whenever I smell lilac it reminds me of days gone by,
The Whit Monday walk around the town
With brass bands and banners on high.
New shoes, new dresses, faces scrubbed bright
Squeaky clean hair, a beautiful sight.
Lilac was pulled from the old Chapel trees -
Filled our baskets, and ribbons to please.
Proudly we marched through the streets of the town
Whether May Queen's attendant or just walking round,
The stop at the Town Hall to sing of our best -
With brass bands resounding, gave us a rest.
We had to get back to the Chapel for tea
Then off to the field for sports it would be.
Running and skipping we gave it a try
If we came a-cropper we tried not to cry
At last it would come to the end of the day,
The lilac had faded, the baskets away
It's strange we we're older the things you recall
When the scent of the lilac blows over the wall.

Joan Milner

NOON AT THE LAKESIDE

The sheen of ice lures me down to the wooded
Hollow. Somewhere between footbridge and thickets
I have crossed a spiritual barrier and welcome
Sequences of reed, rhododendron and bamboo
Framed by the height of oaks and beeches.

In the middle of the waterfowl flocks
A swan pair stand; white ships on a sea
Of glass; apart and each supported by black
Splayed paddles; their waxen plumage and plush
Downy necks edged with golden light.

As if instinctively recognising meridian
The cob arches his wings, raises bill tip
To the sky, gives out eleven singular trumpet
Notes; the swan song finale, a deep resonant
Purr being achieved when the cob lowers his head
And imperceptibly lifts rounded crop.

Each intonation sharply distorts the silence
Soaking into my grateful mind
Along with the east wind's smarting chill
And the awareness that I have looked
In on a wilderness element devoid of all
Human trespass, save that of my eyes.

Keith Taylor

MY TOE

Now I try and rest in my hospital bed,
'That's what you're here for' everybody said.
Rest your 'toe' that's been amputated,
Move down a bed or two - relegated.

I nearly died when I first saw the toe,
It was black and horrible.
I rushed up here, full of fear,
You'll have to come in the doctor said,
Better it's off! - We'll send you to bed.

Three days later - traumatised,
I went on a trolley to theatre three.
Heavens above, is this really me,
Everyone in there I knew
Care assistants, theatre crew.
I used to work here, (didn't I know it),
I was petrified, did I really show it?

I came back with one toe less (nine toes red)
Now I try and rest in my hospital bed.

Janet Dickson

POST OFFICE

Continuous coughing, talking and tutting
The bang of the door continually shutting

The grannies and grandads they gossip together
'It's terrible to have to come out in wet weather'

Mothers they screech at their children who cry
Why can't I have sweets Mummy, why Mummy why?

A young man impatient, he turns the air blue
All the sounds of the local post office queue

Lynn Marsden

JOY

Joy would be sun
and I walking in Vallouris again,
and when I was done
with dimpled pots of green and yellow
I would take the train to Menton beach
to sit on the shingle
when all the holiday folk were gone.

Sometimes the rain,
spattering the tall palms in Juan
would beat in my brain,
and I would ride through the waves
to the Iles de Lerins, to walk
by the weed creamed surf,
under a thickness of pine,
when the holiday folk were gone.

J Harrington

NOVEMBER DAWNS

The paper rustle
of littered leaves
the blustering wind blows harsh,
darkened days
and guarded nights
death lingers on the marsh.

Matted bracken
swiftly wisps
and swallows pierce the air,
formation by
their instincts
no pilot grapples there.

Hedgehog's spikes
no longer shuffle
under cover of the moon,
blackness thickens
her extended realms
that steeps the earth in doom.

The sun lies
still and restful
through winter's icy crow,
till reclaimed
her powers risen
to cajole the spring to glow.

Elizabeth Coop

EAST ANGLIA

Come with me and see the things that I have seen -
Skies that stretch into infinity
Blue as the bell flowers which hide,
Shy as maidens, 'neath the green beech trees
In springtime.

Come with me to hear the music of life,
Urgent its call in the rose-red dawning,
Tranquil in praise for the day now gone
When the evening star candlelights
The quiet meadows.

Come with me and live while yet we may -
So much still to see and do -
But time on wings forever young
Leaves us behind with only memories.
Come with me and live
Ere time has gone.

M I Maggs

ESSENCE OF ALL OUR YESTERDAYS

A scented floral garden
reminiscent of Sundays at Gran's
lavender pouches with little bows
and her lanolin softened hands,

Chalk-dust will always bring
those schooldays into our minds
no running in the corridor
the cost one hundred lines,

Sawdust has an acquired aroma
yet it always brings to thought
those evenings in the circus tent
and where's those red noses we bought.

Nothing smells cleaner or fresher
than a lawn that's newly mowed
memories of charity galas
the procession pounding the road,

Not many can pass a public house
without daydreaming that first drop of ale,
how awful and bitter it tasted
they said it's the pleasure of many a male,

Aftershave a scent for a man
as teenager, a budding Casanova
they took the slogan literally
and splashed the stuff all over,

But fish and chips recall the seaside
the memories I enjoy the most
buckets, spades and donkey rides
and being waited on by a host.

J D Ashton

SEACHANGE

We get off the bus like convicts squinting under open skies.
We take our plastic bags, our cans, our flasks,
our family packs of chocolate melting on their bones of
toffee and stretch tartan rugs on the soft splints of sand
between the rocks. The kids run off, armed with stick-nets
and gum boots, to poke in the winey depths the rock pools.
A few brave souls with swinging pots of belly, their skin
tightening with goose-flesh, take the plunge, grasping the water
with clattering limbs. All day long the halls of cliff echo with
screaming cloud of gulls, and all day we bask beneath the pulsing
dot of sun like burning red lizards; until at last the sky surrenders
and veils her crown of gold. The parents tramp one by one,
chatting, into the pub of red faces - mother, with a light glass
of bubbly and a salt edge of crisp - father, sinking a pint of stout
with a local, a gap-toothed smile of a man with stories of the sea.
Outside, hanging on the last few minutes the children run,
crunching along the shorey shingle with a half-pushed ball
or sand-filled can, kicking clouds of pebble and shell-spit.
But now it's time to go and we load the bus with weary,
glowing bodies, wiping stinging eyes in tingling heads; we leave
behind dots of can and glass, a flurry of papers blotted with
chip grease on the pier, a stain of footprints down the empty beach;
we leave the sky, a black wing of rain rising on its back, we leave
the wind, gathering itself in cold breaths, and we leave the sea,
prowling, its white edges hissing on the jagged dark.

Bill Murphy

BRAVE OAK

Rustling, bustling, glimmering, shimmering
How many years have you seen?
Wind, rain, sun and snow
But what you've seen you never show.
Boys came climbing, dancers singing
For never-ending gifts you're bringing.
Withstanding storms of blazing lightning
Beneath your boughs we found it frightening.
War raged round you as men lay dying
The rain on your leaves hung there crying.
You stand defiant through years of sorrow
Pointing onward to the new tomorrow.
Full of courage, self-healing you seem to be,
Oh what I'd give for the strength of thee!

K Scarfe

THE SNAPSHOT

In my album I have an old snapshot
a picture much cherished by me.
It's faded and creased and torn down one edge
showing you and a child on your knee

I loved you from the beginning
and thought that you'd always be there.
I told you things no-one else heard
and secrets I'd want you to share.

Some evenings we'd sit by the window
the golden sun touching your head.
You'd tell me of times when you were a child
and I'd listen to all that you said.

I wonder if you can remember
the times I would sit on your knee
and put my arms tight around you
but you'd just sit there, passively.

You never could show your affection
for reasons that I never knew.
Some said you were hard, with no feeling
I never believed that was true.

What was it that you didn't tell me?
The something you tried to forget.
You held back so no-one could hurt you
and now it's too late for regret.

But life makes memories dimmer
and now all there's left here to see
is the torn creased picture I have of you
and the child that sat on your knee.

John Bryant

THE CEMETERY

A dark, a lonely scary place
Of which I was afraid,
Bunches of dying daffodils
Across the tombstones laid.

Statues stood like witches
Among the graves of stone,
Snapping twigs and noises
Which chilled me to the bone.

The church was like a prison
The iron gates of black,
And once you walked along the path
You didn't dare look back.

But many years have long-since passed
No longer a little girl
The gates no more are black as night
But shine with gold and pearl.

The snapping twigs are little birds
Nesting in the trees,
The noises are just melodies
Echoing in the breeze.

The statues are of angels
All heavenly in white,
The daffodils like candles
Which burn throughout the night.

The place is filled with sunshine
From which the flowers thrive,
It's not the dead that hurt us
But those who are alive.

Joanne Gough

BY NO MEANS HOMELESS

By no means homeless
Your wasps
Who flew so far
From a foreign country
To build
On an insignificant bush
In a country garden
A delicate home
Of bark-like, architectured beauty.

I saw it there,
Slung between twigs,
Only the wasps movement
Betraying its green presence,
Shaped like a spinning top,
With opening at the base for exits and entrances.

Entranced we were,
Still are, by its skeletal remains.
Apart from a few, persistent, autumnal wanderers
The wasps are dead.
A queen, somewhere, seeks sanctuary
For the winter.
But you have your trophy -
A many layered ball
In subtle browns, greens,
Encasing an hexagonal heart,
Strong in its structure of neatly fitting cells.

A nest, exquisite,
Nurturing so many thousand
Enemies of mankind!

Rosemary Wells

THE ABBEY

Sunset had dyed the clouds behind the hill;
Against their rosy glow stood gaunt, bare trees,
Frozen their sap by nature's wintry rage,
But still they watched, guarding the church and dome
That towered above them, in the sky's expanse.
Even so the abbey's monks, aged and few,
Stand in support around their chosen head,
Who took their vows in the floodtide of youth.
Still their foundation, raised above our town
Its light of prayer and holy living sheds.

Sheila Durbin

WRECK DIVING

Then that was that . . .
We'd given everything
a second inspection, checking the knives
for sharpness, the cylinders full, the O rings in
and O rings spare around the cylinder necks
joking about the wreck deaths the previous week
like fishing for conger in the Deeps.

If you'd said the weather was good
you'd have lied, the weather was better
and the sea clear as jelly; green, cold jelly
recently taken from the fridge,
previously runny, gooey in hot water yesterday,
vortexing around the measuring glass jug
like the sea greasing off the hull of our hard boat . . .

And in the sun you really burnt
not noticing until it burnt
and tingled uncomfortably through your dry-suit
while the dive marshal checked all working parts;
'Breathe, twice. Depth gauge, watch and wait . . .
You're next.' Then sit and wait
kitted up on the side, drugged and out of it

then into it, the turtle shell is a mattress
then let the cold water wrap, absorb like filaments
of glacial string the tropical beach
the sweetness of forbidden skin
and sink and sink the swollen bloom
I see the outline of a wreck beneath us
and think but do not think that it shall keep us.

Anthony le Feuvre

DOWN AND OUT

A whole new experience as on we went,
Making for the Chunnel,
To the upper-deck we were sent,
And down into the Channel Tunnel.

As we set off, it was so smooth,
We knew not we'd made a start,
It was, we thought, all meant to soothe,
Those people of faint heart!

Then we sped along so fast,
And were told we were half way,
But, oh dear, this was not to last,
What were they going to say!

We slowed right down, almost to halt,
Whatever could be wrong,
As we waited to be told the fault,
We tried to sing a song!

But then we gathered speed again,
Yet, once more, there was a stop,
Was there an obstacle in our lane,
Or were we for the chop!

But then we speeded up once more,
Into the light of day,
Round in a circle as we saw,
Nous arrivons à Calais!

Jill M Ronald

OUR CHURCH

There is a church on our estate
Which isn't very old.
It's very modern in design
And unusual to behold.

The hymns and prayers are usual
And most are quite well known.
The cross and lights are made of iron,
And the aisles are all of stone.

Yet when the sun comes creeping in
And people therein trod,
There is an atmosphere descends -
You're in the House of God!

Dorothy Lloyd

CLAYPIT WOOD

Here in the hollow lies a legacy
of last year's spent and crumbling
leaves, pierced by bluebell shoots

and pale dog mercury.
The stark trees range along the rim,
old mottled trunks yellow as winter

seas running in over sand.
Somewhere a woodpecker is drumming
a dead branch, and a far-off cockerel crows.

There is no scent. The pale sun,
rinsed by northern winds, seems powerless
to liberate the faintest whiff.

One sees so far in February, when
crystal air is sharp as the memory
of an old man's spring.

Alison Vernon

ALONG THE RIVER NEB

In the warm and balmy evening,
where the river winds its way,
I strolled along the gorse-strewn path
and breathed the scent of sun on hay.
Little sounds were all around me,
making silence deeper still -
the flurry of a startled bird,
the creaking from the watermill.
I listened to the tinkling music
of the river, crystal clear,
babbling over dappled pebbles
ere it reached the man-made weir.
I heard a tiny, popping noise,
it came from bursting pods of broom
scattering their contents o'er the earth,
preparing next year's golden bloom.

The meadowland across the stream
was full of chirping insect sounds
where silverweed, dog daisies, vetch
played hide and seek 'mid grassy mounds.
O'ergrown by pampas grass and reeds,
a long-forgotten creek I found,
where childhood games I used to play,
away from grown-ups' sight and sound.

A sudden flash of memories came
with many a reminiscent smile,
as I recalled such happy days,
when I was young on Mona's Isle.

Maisie Sell

CRAB COTTAGE. PRESENT AND PAST

I wandered down the country lane, along the riverside
And came upon the cottage that was tended, once, with pride;
It's empty and neglected now: the grass is straggling high,
The crazy paving's sprouting weeds, the lily pond is dry,
There still exists a wooden shed (the door is loose and 'wonky')
That housed the family's transport, namely Muriel - the donkey!
A pole which held a tethered goat is lying on its side,
The chicken coop is empty and its door is open wide;
Perhaps potatoes grow there still beside the podded peas?
Well, anyway, small pears are growing on the orchard's trees.

The city seems so far away from this sweet country scene,
Evocative of earlier times, unhurried and serene;
The gurgling of a little brooklet calls to mind the sound
Of happy children's laughter as they played and danced around:
How very little time there was for carefree fun and play,
And yet they seemed much happier than children are today;
How basic was their schooling, yet how eagerly they learned,
How willingly they worked at home so praises would be earned;
Eleven children graced the cottage, oh so long ago,
But only I am left now. That is rather sad, you know.

Rosemary Y Vandelt

LEVEL WITH EARTH
(To EWL)

Backed by rock
and underlain by sand,
overpinned by stars
in a desert land,
cool-kissed by breath of night,
moon-mazed, I lie
level with the earth
and lorded by the sky.

Chris Moat

A Remembered Place

I know too much
this place

It hurts to see
the stairs you came down
that very last day

It torments to walk
the floor we sat on
or touch the bench
on which we scratched
our teasing rimes of play

This place does waken
my mortification

I know too much
to live it again

The crest we surfaced on
has gone
and long departed

L Simcock-Daisy

COLD

Cold.
Air gasping,
Goose pimpling,
Cold.
Bone freezing,
Chest slapping,
Cold.

K Axon

MOONLIT MEADOW

A life untouched by man's great sorrow
Is the life above no one can borrow
Withdraw from this world, fly far away
Into a land, follow this way

Moonlit meadow is what I see
Swaying flowers in the peaceful breeze
Gentle sigh, breath of honest air
Simple, you have been taken there

The moon casts over a pale blue colour
Supplying the river with woundless cover
No sign of madness is the mystery
In this land of all tranquillity

Here your mind can start to roam
And serenity will be the tone
That small moment will have such meaning
In a world which forfeits healing

Soon this time will fade away
Into reality, you don't have to stay
You cannot live without a dream
Hold fast to your moonlit meadow

Jorjana Franklin

STARRY SKY

Timeless sentinels unlimited beyond vision's grasp
Their twinkling lights reaching earth from ages past
Intriguing aura of mystery, space travelled where
Perhaps reminding us to consider great distances compare
Filling our minds with wonderment beyond infinity
Realise humbly our own earthly station interim fast

Gazing skyward provided clear conditions viewing reveal
A kaleidoscope of limitless stars, illuminated patterns arrayed
Dwarfing our earthly pedestal our humility should concede
Our platform unique space found permits worthy need
Perhaps future years may offer some limited space explore
Or otherwise we accept human limitations satisfied displayed.

Intriguing thoughts may pass our human observance to offer
Distances beyond normal perception, relayed across light years
Limitless to explain, easy conception, further hard to believe
Could be destined of true reality, with reflection, our limits conceive
Destiny will fulfil, our earthly sights, further horizons attain
We must keep realistic perspective, avoid overdone, tragic fears.

Concede with common-sense a realisation, ourselves unique
Provided future years do not indicate life further afield
Even so our earthly existence seem beyond pure chance
Destiny must have created a happening no fluke down glance
Millions of stars and planets, seem beyond lucky forming
More like a supernatural intelligence, spirit guided eternal shield.

F J Carradus

A Windy Day On The Norfolk Broads

Our boat was anchored by the reeds on Hornsey Mere.
Drowsily we awoke, stretched ourselves: yawned, and peered
Through half-closed eyes at moorhens swimming fussily.
A pale watery sun shone down through parted clouds.
A cold breeze ruffled the surface of the water.
Clutching mugs of coffee we emerged on deck.
Suddenly there was a whoosh and clatter of wings
As wild ducks flew upwards out of the golden mist.
Soon we were chugging along the grey waterway.
The wind had freshened. White clouds skimmed the airy blue.
Cattle grazed contentedly in the marshy fields.
Flocks of black starlings whirled across the morning sky.
A storm-tossed heron flapped slowly down the river.
The leafless trees were bent against the autumn gales.
The scene was a Constable painting brought to life.
We stood hugging the wheel in our breeze-filled jackets;
Feeling exhilarated, rejuvenated,
In this wind-driven, cloud-riven Norfolk landscape.

J S Maidwell

UNEXPECTED

Levitate towards the sky,
not knowing if your mind will survive.
Mystical magic I can feel.
The apocalypse is here and truly real.
My soul is the protective keeper but is my mind in evil danger?
Memories ablaze in my heart, never knowing to stay, or depart.
As I feel my saddened emotions, I concoct my elaborate potion.

Myasser Ashraf (15)

THE GARDEN

The blooming flower bud
Keeping its fragrant petals
Slightly ajar
Ulterior motive in mind . . .
Beckoning the bee
To bathe in and taste
The oozing sweet nectar
The divine experience!

The succulent ripe fruit
Eager to burst open
The fountain of sweet juice
To the lips
Yearning to suck and savour
The divine essence.

Anand Deshpande

UNTITLED

This tall, handsome little person, 18 months old,
studies every feature of his new brother's face,
nose, eyes, mouth;
their eyes meeting.
Slowly he bends over the little moving miracle,
nose to gentle nose, saying
'Hello'
Big brother, whose loving parents,
a mere breath - time ago,
had whispered the same to him for the first time,
smiled and turned to play with his new car.
All surrounded by unlimited love, justly content.

Helen Harlow

EVEN WOLVES CAN DREAM

Music softly playing
        a haunting melody
Tearing at my heartstrings
Transporting me on phantom wings
        to lands across the sea
Lands so rich in minerals
        of myriad shape and hue
Shades of turquoise, brown and purple
Red and yellow, green and blue

Music dreams are made of
        when worlds are torn apart
Soaring over mountain tops
        its message to impart . . .
Let Nature rule unbounded
        allow all creatures to run free
Leave this inherent miracle
        for all the world to see

And still the music flows along
        in poignant harmony
Echoing through the valleys
        to its final destiny
Bringing hope to all wild animals
        and a message to mankind . . .
Only you can save this planet
        do it now, or you may find
That it could be lost forever
        like the ripples on a stream
And the hopes of nature shattered . . .
        for even wolves can dream

Joan Galpin

NIGHT STORM

Skeletal fingers tap on windowpane
And scrape, like jagged fingernails
Upon the peace of slumber, to explode
The mind to winter's hell.
Hidden rafters creak and groan.
The door, ajar, gives swing, as if
Aboard a storm-tossed ship.
The old brass bed - though strong
Trembles like a frightened dog.

Crisp, clean sheets grow chill
As devil's mighty breath, filters through
Each crack and split of wall decay
Like shafts of ice.
Satan's witches, howl outside
And steer, close by the window
Hard astride their flying hazel brooms.

So passed one night, of darkest velvet
Until, first grey of morn
Gave silhouette to naked trees.
Then stillness, so like the dead
Grew hushed, with softest whimper
Dismissed itself, and limped away.

Henry J Green

Dorset Gap

Trees in shady fields
Where seasons meet
Butterflies and beetles and bees
A gap in time
Untouched by history

A painted lady breezes
Through purple pyramids
Vervain and valerian and vetch
Protected from progress
Then and now and always

Kersty Strong

The Circle Of Time

The seasons their assigned Time run,
Each bringing a beauty all its own,
As personal as a fingerprint
The fingerprint of Time.

Which shall be first?
Your favourite you may choose
In nature there's no end,
A circle of Time as on life goes.

Spring - the first?
The first awareness, the awakening of growth.
Of lambs, of leaves, of greener fields,
The busy Time of Youth.

Summer, and air hangs hot over the land
An almost tangible thing.
With a timeless sense of tranquil days
- Lulling the unwary to think Time forever stays.

Autumn when the first slight frost
Brings blushes to the leaves, and aloft
A haze of woodsmoke drifts in the air,
Now for the Time of sleep nature must prepare.

Winter, below its mantle hides,
Transforms the shapes of all from sight,
In pale sunshine on sparkling white.
Sunshine will vanquish winter's icicle
Completing the whole *Time Circle*.

E Walker

THE LITTLE THINGS

Stray memories, fond reminiscence,
Ribbon in her hair,
Joy in her step,
On a cold concrete clicking,
The twinkle in her eye,
The feel of her touch,
Her rose coloured smile,

Strange voices, my memory jolting,
Forgotten snippets of conversation,
Lonely smiles on sandy beaches,
Filling my shoes, flying, whipping,
Snatching my breath away.

Lucid waves rolling, my eyes deceiving,
Purple blue crashing at my feet,
Gulls calling,
Lost souls,
In a holocaust's lonely wake,

Silent dreams laughing, invisible hands caressing,
Suddenly awakening,
Stricken and blue,
Eyes hopelessly searching,
Endlessly finding,
Memories of you.

P D Taylor

A Sanctuary True

Winding lanes and farmland scenes
Embrace the route to Bowness.
Upon arrival you park with such ease,
And *free* at the harbour's edge.
Take in the air as you stroll round the lake
And chance for a real dairy ice;
(Not 'shaving foam' found in the inner city),
All flavours won't fail to entice.
Be careful - the swans will be out in their dozens,
Bowness is a sanctuary true.
Intending to lighten your lunch box of treats,
They greet; as you come in to view!
Further along, for an hour of your time:
A cruise on the steamboat is fine.
Or on to the High Street for endless supply,
Of curio before you dine.
Distinguished restaurants and pizza shacks
You'll see them all in your stride,
And after the saunter; a well-earned rest,
In a vacant spot on the hillside.
Amusement donated by puppeteer dolls,
Playing merry classics in Top 'n' Tail dress.
And as evening approaches, the journey back home,
With memories gained of the beautifulness
Of this heart-warming place to be.

Katrina M Greenhalf

MOORS IN WINTER

It's wintertime on the moorland heath
The grassy tufts are yellowed on the mossy peat
The wind is restless and never ceases
And damp mist clings to the wandering sheep's fleeces

Like lost souls aimlessly ambling on the hillsides cloaked in mist
Their woolly heads foraging for turf which might be crisp
But finding none, content themselves to the thin yellow strands of grass
As they tread the stony pathways, so narrow that two can't pass

On the craggy slopes of the higher peaks in crevices they huddle
Young lambs beside their mother's form, eagerly awaiting suckle
And the ewes give answer to their cries in deep successive bleats
Giving the lambs protection, lest they fall in gentle sleep

When in the early evening the sun has sunk so low
And splashes the sky with vermilion, fading to a rosy glow
Then the ewes and lambs fall silent as night creeps o'er the sky
And slumber slowly claims them, closing each bleary eye

Elaine Goodman

EAST BERLIN

Dear battered city
Torn by East and West
One feels such pity
For you have no rest.
Eastern built buildings
Brought to rubble now
While your politicians
To the West still bow.
Dear battered city
Out of horror comes
Love, peace and friendship
As the Reichtag dons
Fantasy clothing
Shimmering in the night
Dear battered Berlin
You're going to be - alright!

Hazel Browne

BLUEBELLS

The first of May is my birthday
And my special birthday treat,
Is to go and see the bluebells
In abundance round my feet.

A carpet of blue, so beautiful,
As far as the eye can see,
It's Mother Nature at her best,
In all her majesty.

As a child, I would gather them,
But now I'm quite content,
To stand and gaze and marvel
And absorb the wonderment.

J M Rowe

SOUTH DEVON

One pretty week in May
bluebells overflow into the sea
rampant banks, planted earlier
rush to come out as though
to share our holiday.

Baby oak leaves, pink of
chaffinch breast, warms up
the hedge, speedwells soft
spread. The poor and rich
orchids and plantains mix
the sun keeps open house.
Cows crossing, hold up
the traffic, great udders
swinging, will anyone ever
go short again? Each cliff top
path leads to another
there's a Dolphin, Royal Oak,
Sloop Inn, all sell Bass
and fat crab sandwiches.

Driving back from Plymouth
road divides tall fields
trees arch our way as though
a king is due to come this way
an occasional surprise
of oilseed, playing at gold
glisters among the green.
Notice faded primroses
and late leftover violets
fall back, to let, the
bluebells have their day.

E Eveleigh

LANDSCAPE

I remember, I remember,
And still I see you there,
Against the dark grey landscape,
With rain so very near.

I saw today in sunshine,
The very self-same place,
Remembering only,
The shadows on your face.

I kissed you then, remember?
So I now forever see,
The place you stood in sadness,
Changed to happiness for me!

Mary Hughes

A Tribute To Those Who Died
(25th September 1940 at Filton, Bristol -
Bristol Aeroplane Company)

That day was bathed in sunshine and mellow fruitfulness.
Light upon green meadows, emerald loveliness,
But those of us who did survive
Will remember that noon-day hour.
As the second air raid warning sounded from the tower,
Like a flash of summer lightning
Planes bore down on us from the blue.
I remember each and every one of us in shelter 622.
        Noise and smell of sulphur,
        Hell descending from the skies,
        As we prayed and sat there trembling,
        Our shelter cracked from side to side.

So today at St Peter's, Filton, the service so well portrayed,
Hymns so aptly chosen and words of comfort said,
My heart was full to bursting, so proud was I to be
Among those who paid a tribute to that tragic memory.
        So for those who are left let's be thankful
        Not knowing what the future will hold
        But I'm sure we all have our memories
        And it's we who are left who will grow old.

M Dury

OUR DEAR RIVER VER

She started life at Kensworth Lynch -
a glisten in the dell
but soon she found a bubbly sound
to water Markyate Cell;
and oft she heard Christina's thoughts
as on her way our rill
had gathered heart to greet her ward -
the homestead on the hill.
She gave her name to Verlamstead
(the homestead on the Ver)
which soon became the Flamstead name
as later times prefer.
She told the tale how Henry Eighth
sent Edward to get well,
but neither she nor finest air
could halt the looming knell,
And so our treasure gathered strength
to wash the Roman road
o'er Friar's Wash, and then she, proud
through reeded valley flowed.
At Redbourn now she slowed her pace
to tell the ancient tale -
Amphibalus with Alban's cloak -
Saw might of Rome prevail.
She then more stately pushed her way
to turn the water mill
until she came to Verulam
to tell how, on a hill
beside her banks the martyr died:
the hero of our race,
and how our great St Albans town
grew round this hallowed place.

But now our river too has died,
she's killed in part by man;
looks forward till her daughter springs
will help her flow again.

Owen Edwards

MEMORIES

I walk into the empty room,
Why the sense of doom and gloom?
I walk out through another door,
And find myself crawling across the floor.

There is no light to be seen,
Everything is a haze of green.
Why do I feel so sad and cold,
What do these old walls behold?

Memories flicker through my mind,
If only an answer I could find.
Thoughts race back to another day,
I see myself, but am so far away.

Another world I have entered in,
Now my mind is in such a spin.
Flashes remind me of another time,
Was that the clock-tower I heard chime?

I open my mouth and scream with fear,
Yes it's true - I almost died in here.
My kidnappers have gone, I can now escape,
And go to the police and report my rape . . .

Gwen Walsh

BIRD BRAIN FEATHER WAIT

a slap-happy union of barren flagpoles was jacking itself off
all over the city
I desperately needed a quill to keep up with myself as Ghent unfolded
its over-done-it-again self
got one finally and like a main line plumber I let it tap into the vain
waste pipe of my thought
I stood in the street outside the writers' shop
       and like a gutful of vomit my long-denied words puked out
for twenty minutes I stood there in the gutter as my guilty star
splashed over the paper void
passers-by were shocked and stunned
I could see the front page 'Man Given Tasty Sentence For Taking
              Unsavoury Phrases from Life's Literary Banquet'
mothers whisked away their frightened children
dogs stopped halfway through a lamppost piss and yelped off limping
Oh the impotence of words was unsettling everything
cafés closed their doors and pontious church bells started to wring
their pilot hands
finally it was over
our feathered ones could once more take to the air
       or proceed to peck at seeds sown by well-meaning idiots
in London you can do bird just for going against the grain
I shooed myself away
but just hung around with the other grounded flyers
here comes the one called Byron
he went from pigeon-toe to club-foot Don Juan Childe-like Hour of
Idleness when he was How old
I whispered in his Shelley-like
'I'm a bird-brained poet to boot'
but he cleared off
to top a flagpole's ecstasy

oh dear oh dear

Bryan William Green

THE STREAM

Down the lane, all white and cream
a row of cottages, face the stream.
The sides are steep, the water shallow
and ducks feed there, amongst the mallow.
An ancient wall beside the stream
encompasses the churchyard, green,
where roses in the summer grow,
their petals blown to float below.

The church was built and made to last,
to serve the village, in times past.
The door of oak kept out invaders,
Vikings, Jutes and Danish raiders.
And over all, the keep stands high,
its ruins reaching to the sky.
When Normans came in this direction
they built the castle, for protection.

From here, a narrow street drops down,
into the centre of the town,
where oak-beamed houses proudly stand,
some of the oldest in the land.
Over the bridge, beside the green,
the path leads back, towards the stream,
And down the lane the ducklings come
behind their mother, one by one.

Jan Pollard

THE VISITOR

The morning sun burst through the clouds,
Slipped silently and unannounced
Through a window into a room,
Spreading light, displacing gloom.

The lady quietly sitting there
Was completely unaware
Of the radiance of his light,
She who from birth had not known sight.

Blind she was but not neglected
By the visitor, so unexpected.
Suddenly his rays caressed her,
His warmth enfolded and possessed her.
Then she knew him, knew his name.
She smiled to say she was glad he came.

Ruth Suffolk

THE WINDOW

I like to go past this particular window.
It could look forlorn and down.
But it is a rich illumination
in a cheap and cheerful town.

It could look mean and penniless taut,
but waves of muslin mantle the bay.
It is a rich giving of a gentle thought.
On a cold, empty, gas-meter day.

This promenade of curtain'd whiteness
gives the street its washing-line day.
A photograph could snap the bleakness.
History's stand against decay.

My memory walks me past your door.
The texture of my thought is like
her hands that smoothed the linen cloth.
A simple natural thing, done right.

Susan Roberts

A Bridge At Dusk

Weeping willows by the Thames river,
Soothe me, mould me, make me quiver,
Swans glide gracefully 'neath arched rustic walls,
Pretentious, and elegant, like dazzling snowballs.

Boats, like phantoms, sailing mutely,
No panic, no hustle, the essence of beauty.
A breeze, a stir, a gentle whiff.
Then out of sight like a wispy nymph.

Feelings enhanced, feelings rifled,
Tension, stress and pressure stifled.
Renewed in body, renewed in spirit,
In a spot where earth and Heaven cement, Henley.

Mary Quinlan

WHEN I REMEMBER

When I remember
Being at Shieldaig -
I think of long, light
Saturated summer evenings -
A light intense and lingering,
As the sun endured
Extending day into the night, and
The sea sounded
A slow, steady, soothing rhythm
Against the stony shore -
So that, just for that moment,
The whole world appeared to rest
And take its ease,
Upon this cusp of perfect peacefulness.

George B Burns

Oban's Bay

Looking out across the bay
This is where I long to stay
Watching boats go sailing past
Wishing they didn't go so fast

Sitting on Oban's rocky shore
Wishing I could stay for evermore
Watching Mull in the mist hide
Having a seal sat by my side

Watching fishermen unload their catch
Seeing an old tar strike a match
Thoughtfully his pipe he lights
I wonder how often he has seen that sight

Now I must go away
From the place where I want to stay
I will miss Oban's rocky shore
Until I can return once more

Katrina Holland

DAYDREAMS

I dream a dream of yesteryear.
Of days gone by
         with little fear.
Of traffic seen,
         not being raced.
An air breathed,
         not chemically laced.
My eyes wonder,
         upon terraced rows.
Little houses, cobbled streets
Worker, hurrying
         tapping clogs on feet.
A delicious smell of baking bread,
         rises to my waiting nose.
Overcoming the odour,
         of my Lancashire rose.
For this dream, is man as child.
Heady days, when kids were fair
         a little wild.
When pubs had snugs, sold dark mild.
For this is Salford, of long ago.
As I daydream, who will know!

H Livesey

Kirk Fell

Such ginger light and moonfaced pride and,
glistening crags and upthrusting altitude

Such ice-cream snow and grassy wafers, on
the lights over lowland fields

Such lonely skyline unfrequented by people,
and lonely heart above the cosy church

Such heather and bracken and scree,
open to the dale head.

Such simple love and golden light,
to warm my eyes and bring delight.

Michael James Fuller

SKEGGY

Off the Lincoln scarp -
Suddenly the sea - land smoothes ambiguous to left and right
Flat water-colour strokes of field fen to a faint horizon,
Thumb - smudged where greys and greyer, greys collude
Until it seems we drive forever into sea - sky.
Hopeful a child heart leaps for the wave in every turn,
The folded marsh ceaseless unfolds to enticed chagrin.
The city left, long left the dull same - seeming streets;
Where is the wet washed beach waiting for our paddling pails,
The picnic dunes with silk - warmed hollows for our limbs?
Look! The water tower inked upon an opalescent mood,
A semaphore defining fen, sea fringe and sky.
Beat on the coach glass, shout and stamp, we're here!
Freed sand - filled shoes run down the ribbed and wrinkled beach,
Which like a spread wet raincoat glimmers in the milk - hazed sun:
And still the thin, froth fussing sea recedes to a brush-stroke.
We chase it flap, flop, flapping down the quivering sand
To stumble, stagger, fall gasping from the breathless cold
Into the sea at last, furtive, brown, salt stinging, sly.
All day it spends in creeping here and there while children shout,
As our day dies it hides the sun, fuming and hissing
At the edge of town and we go home across the wide pale-painted land,
The sense of loss and leaving but the first of many.

Tony Bowers

ISLE OF EIGG 1984

Without roads, there seems no direction
or future - just a past
Immediate and immemorial
In symbols of personal despair
Rusting cars and emptied cans.
The old few bent by the relentless wind
Sigh and shrug.
The land alone is rich;
Tear-stained by streams,
Now cloud covered
Now ravaged by rabbits.
The young, chins reflected in kingcups
Bloom in their desolate legacy.
But there is true perspective
In the wide skies and an escape
For birds that call and wing
With fighter jets
Over a nuclear-wasted sea.

Edwina Vardey

WHEN THE SUN CROSSES THE CELESTIAL EQUATOR

The equinoxes seem to be the most difficult part of the year,
One is at the end of one's physical tether after winter
With weather changes so abominably.
Just to bask in a sunshine of almost summer-like power
Yet, the outward token of spring is here!
Almond blossom, prunus, daffodils and bird-chewed crocuses,
Yes, even stock in bloom - a genuine flower of summer.

Then I seem to crumple up, with an inner sort of tiredness,
These dark months don't help;
What with recurrent fog and mild dripping days.
Not that I am one to grumble about the weather,
It is so difficult when it comes after days of frost
As you're all dressed up, for a continuance of cold frosty days
Yes, the equinoxes, are the most difficult part of the year.

Judith Anne Carmichael

Culloden Memorial

Finished in Nairn
swimming, picnic and ices
Culloden was an off-chance
something to do with time to kill.

Odd that we should find ourselves
deep in heather beneath dull grey clouds
thinking of sleet in April,
a diminishing dream, charismatic pretence
and butchery.

And how stones may last and flowers fade
after religion, ritual and vainglory
have driven men to fight.

John Clarke

SUNSET IN THE TREES

The blue blends into the
    honeydew
that bathes the sky in gold
And I release the pain
Soaring strength
when I left my eyes - high
Grace. I call my children

How did this red
    happen
      and
        land

So beautiful in the trees
The beauty is precise
It warms the cold
Explicit second.
Naked nerve
but now . . .

      Silent space
        and silent space
        and silent space.

Sarah Hardy

SKYLINES

Sky screen above the sweep of the flyover,
Near-silhouettes and darkening blue,

I drive the city in search of skylines,
        and never knew until now.

Beryl Stockman

BELFAST

Today smells like the kind of day
A bomb could go off
Today feels like the type of day
A cease-fire could end
Today tastes like the sort of day
A friend could be knee-capped
Today sounds like Belfast

Today smells like the kind of day
A bonfire could be lit
Today feels like the type of day
Armoured cars are stoned
Today tastes like the sort of day
That killings are sectarian
Today sounds like Belfast

Today smells like the kind of day
Talks become stagnant
Today feels like the type of day
Orange men march united
Today tastes like the sort of day
Nationalists stand behind blockades
Today sounds like Belfast

Francis McFaul

Busy Café

I like to sit in a small cafe
With good food set in front of me,
But I'm also a budding poet
Studying rest of community.

Two ladies chatting over coffee,
On family, and world situation;
If they could only have their way
They could set right all of creation!

Doting dad with tiny kids,
All boisterous and full of fun;
He only gently chided,
And then the havoc began!

A young, loving couple,
They've food in front of them too;
But do they eat much of it?
They're keener on billing and coo!

Patient waitress is trying to serve
Fussy customer, who is there to dine,
But do any of the menu items
Really suit anyone quite so fine?

There's the quiet type engrossed in book
Does she eat much of her meal?
I think she eventually finishes,
But the book had great appeal!

Such varied types in a cafe;
What a hectic day it must be,
I just don't know how they cope,
It wouldn't do for me!

Marjorie Cowan

BRIGHTON CAROUSEL

Round and round and round
Goes the carousel,
Horses bobbing and glittering
In the sparkling light.

One child going forward,
Turning and turning,
Going forward but turning
Out of the light,
Into the dark
Against a backdrop
Of the sparkling sea.

The constant up and down,
Going forward but turning,
Light followed by dark by light,
Has an uneasy feeling,
Too similar to our own lives
For comfort.

Chris Malcomson

TRIUMPH OF THE SPIRIT

The castle speaks of strength in
Unyielding stone.
Centuries have not eroded an atmosphere of
Hostile force,
Its tangible power instils a
Sense of awe.
Created to subdue it overpowered but
Did not defeat.
Nestled against the walls are houses made of
Stones from the ramparts.
A foreign yoke did not break their spirit for the
People are still here,
Tenacious and stubborn as true Celts who have
Retained their culture and
Go about their mundane lives as the
Red Dragon flies on the tower.

Mair H Thomas

Winter's Memory

I shall never forget, -
No, though I live to be old,
And the war is a long while past,
And all the world is new:
A shiny morning will set
My mind in a hidden fold,
And I shall dream at the last
Of a sky incredibly blue,
Of sunlight on sands that are wet
In a cove cut off from the cold;
And my eyes will follow, with thought aghast,
The trail twelve fighters flew.

Joyce Barton

UNTITLED

To this day, I still see him as he leant against the church gate
while I shivering and trembling watched him wait.
My eyes roamed over his attire searching for the
weapon I was told he carried.
To me he was nothing but a stranger.

He leant on his bicycle, looking tall and strong.
His face seemed calm, expectant not at all offensive.
How *could* he harm this fruit of his loin.

But still I grew uneasy.
I feared his silence, feared his stance.
And wondered, would he ever take my life?

Just 25 minutes he lived in a village very like mine.
9 years before having taken my mother for his bride.
Then came a parting of the ways . . . she returned to her
mother's house.
And he forbidden to set eyes on the daughter he claimed he loved.

I crouched behind an alabaster stone, in fear of
the knife that *had* to be hidden somewhere
I aimlessly twirled in my mouth a golden locket. His christening gift.
It was the third time he tried to see this daughter by his wife.

After an age, I heard him sigh before he finally wheeled his bike,
prepared to pick up the threads of his life.

While I . . . I ran trembling home and bared my soul to the gran
I adored.
Finally aged 26, I searched and found him.
But it was too late to fulfil those childish dreams, and I
am haunted by unfulfilled memories that in my mind continually wind.
For those happy times we could have shared if he had only persevered.
I am saddened for what could have been with my father once so tall,
handsome and lean.

Jay Hendricks

THIS PLACE IS . . . ?

I woke with a start
a haze in my head.
A dim lit room
and in a strange bed!
I lay in a box,
the walls curtained in cream.
The place was so sterile.
Could this be a dream?

'Could this place be Heaven?'
A little voice said,
'Or is this really
what it's like to be dead?
Or could this be a set
like I've seen on TV
and I'm getting paid
for what's happening to me?'

Then ever so quickly
recollection came back,
and my mind started racing
clickety clack!
'How long have I been here?
How did I arrive?
Who got me into A and E
to help me survive?'

Bill Hogg

THE HOSPITAL

The smell of antiseptic, lingers in the air,
Echoed sounds of people groaning, some are in despair.
Dried up blood on tissues, abandoned on the floors.
Doctors rushing past us disappear through rubber doors.

Casualties on trolleys queued up in the hall,
Wheelchair patients waiting for their number call.
Nurses doing all they can to see to everyone,
Casualty is over crowded, but there's more to come.

Bandages and plaster-casts and crutches by the score,
X-rays, stitches, tetanus jabs and many, many more.
Doctors doing overtime to cure the sick and ill,
Giving patients wonder drugs, brown bottles full of pills.

Theatres always busy, surgeons dressed in green,
They work with dedication, they work within a team.
An operation's over it was a great success,
And everyone is happy, relieved by all the stress.

Sometimes things are different, was nothing they could do,
Resuscitation didn't work, the end of life was through.
Breaking news to families and saying that they've gone,
Is the hardest thing for anyone, but sadly life goes on.

Lesley Dearman

GLIMPSES OF INDIA

Night rolls over and opens shuttered day,
banishing deep shadows in rosy light,
nudging waking doorways, as women pray
in chalky devotions patterned bright.
Polished children clasping books and breakfast,
share dirt roads with meandering bullocks.
Painted cartwheels groan, labouring past
bougainvillaea girls bearing heavy crocks.
The day warms in noisy cacophony,
klaxons, loudspeakers, voices stun the air.
Outstretched hands plead in hope and urgency,
silent beauty hides within courtyards rare,
land of palaces, wealth and poverty,
Temples, faith and saffron humility.

Shirley Johnson

SHOW BIRDS

In my tiny urban garden,
The birds present a show,
An everyday performance,
Especially in the snow.
A small bird table is centre stage,
With nuts hanging from a bough,
Where acrobatic tomtits,
Trapeze and make a bow.
A smartly dressed elegant magpie,
In suit of velveteen,
Makes a two-point landing, then,
Struts proudly from the scene.
From an apple tree comes robin,
A long legged blushing beau,
He takes a large crust in his beak,
Then to his nest will go.
There's a wren and cheeky chaffinch,
And sparrows at the feast,
And a mottled chested missel thrush,
A warbling song artiste.
All the acts that appear today,
Are performed in mute and mine,
The singing and the music is,
For spring and summertime.

Brian O'Brien

MORNING WALK IN KUŞADASI - TURKEY

The hot sun makes the tourists frown.
I pass the last hotel - facing the sea
Before the road sweeps away from the town.
I meet the woman who was on the plane and she tells me
Her daughter has danced in the disco on the hill, till dawn.
Boy on the hotel verandah shook a tablecloth, it fluttered
In the shadow briefly, like the wings of a startled swan.
At the causeway café, the locals swim, the driver of the van clattered
The empty cola bottles. While high on the hill the disco lights, hung
Like unripe fruit up in the branches. I watch the bitter-lemon ocean
While peace and the smell of the trees and the harsh notes the cicadas have sung
Is in my ears. An old man approaches waving his hands in a side-ways motion
He talks in Turkish; I do not understand and give him money,
He walks away amongst the squat palm trees on the promenade
As I hear visitors ask to sit at a table where it is not so sunny.
I go back to my hotel; the dust has been swept away. I drink a lemonade.

Heather Walker

CORNISH DREAM

Little sprawling sunlit town
beside the gleaming sea
winding cobbles, pink washed walls
crazy steps and Cornish cream tea.
Ice-cream sellers and bingo halls
boats drawn up on a tiny beach
sea weed smell and fish and chips
gulls that flap and nod and screech
salt that dries upon the lips.
Cold fog that forms and silent slips
round the towns, harbours and cliffs
muffles all as it waits, and then
meets the sun and dissolves again.

Amy Oldham

SUMMER GARDEN

My garden is bright with flowers,
That bloom in the sun and the showers.
There are roses, carnations and hollyhocks tall,
A blue periwinkle covers the wall,
And daisies grow on the lawn.

There's an old sink I use as a planter,
The cat has claimed for her bed,
She curls herself up in the afternoon sun,
There's a plant where she's got her head,
Near the lawn where the daisies grow.

The fish in the pond swim lazily round,
A gentle splash is their only sound,
While the dove who's built her nest in a tree,
Coos from the rooftop endlessly,
While the daisies grow on the lawn.

Evening primroses glow in gathering dusk,
Filling the air with the scent of musk,
And a little hedgehog late at night,
Will search for food by the moon's pale light,
On the lawn where the daisies grow.

Jean Roughton

THE WIND THAT SHAKES THE BARLEY

The wind in the barley
Sounds almost like water,
The way it waves
Through the forest of stalks
Is beautiful,
Changing the form and colour,
Stirring memories in me
That are bittersweet
Of all the places I have lived
And watched the barley move.

Michael Thorpe

Untitled

On the beach we stir, naked at summer
This is so gorgeous, we're laid here together
With our soft flesh we melt into each other
Beneath the warm and tender sun
We're in our hiding place
Our nude joy is endless bliss
It's total love is this.

James Slater

UPON THE HILLS

Upon the hills, covered in a layer of mutability
Contemplative, lying amidst the natural vegetation
Staring at the night sky with profound anticipation
Carving solitude, away from the toxic, twentieth century
A mind blurred by the power of vivid, translucent imagery

Wraith-like, a shadow bathed only in soft moonlight
Dreamscapes meandering through a fertile imagination
Awaiting the first step on the path of transgression
Conceptual visions of ecstasy begin to take flight
Silently praying for the pitch blackness to ignite

Without warning, the sky explodes in a luminous caress,
The hills are illuminated with a brilliant crimson-gold flame
The mortal observe the beauty and whispers her wondrous name
In awe, he screams as he views perfection; perpetual and peerless
And as she fades, he sits, cross-legged, on the tears of his
                                                    goddess.

Steven J Smith

Grandmother's Kitchen

Grandmother's kitchen was cosy and bright
Filled with all things that would delight
A little girl (and that was me)
When I visited Sundays for afternoon tea.
The table spread with lacy cloth
And serviettes like creamy froth
Placed in little silver rings
And china plates, such pretty things,
Sandwiches cut into small triangles
The sugar bowl filled with grains like Spangles,
She would pour the tea into delicate cups
And say 'Eat what you like and quietly sup'
Then she would take from a large tin, a cake
That earlier she had managed to bake.
Chocolate, Maderia or ginger spice
Each variety was always nice.
Then when we finished and cleared away
Her box of jewellery she'd display,
There were beads of crystal and coral too
A sapphire ring, such a beautiful blue,
Dangling earrings and brooches galore
Bracelets and baubles by the score
Velvet headbands with feathers rare
That she wore around her hair
When she was younger and went to a dance
Where she met grandfather, just by chance.
Time has passed and she is no more
But on Sundays my grandchildren come through
                                          the door
And I do for them what she did for me
In the kitchen where we have afternoon tea.

Poppy Meredith

Mablethorpe's Challenge To My Refusal To Gamble

Rope-lights flish-flash, with aggressive
Speed, to slay my inhibition,
And my gambling resistance.
Sense knows jackpots are recessive,
Dodging limits of ambition.

In one squatting slot-machine, coins
Jostle one another round.
Not one single one slides over
That damned edge! Coarse cheers abound
As a hapless 50p joins
Three more, in a hang-over.

Gillian Fisher

RAIN AT WEIRWOOD RESERVOIR

The water at Weirwood,
Flurried by the wind,
Is a grey breath, from an open mouth,
Dimmed in a catacomb of mist.

Wild birds that call,
Make echoes spin this melancholy day.
The darkened ends of winter
Toss and worry round the curling wind.

Rain shades the fading day,
The reservoir, a staring eye,
Sees dark grey clouds,
Hide aquamarine and blue.

Margaret Gibian

VIENNA

Only Vienna can reach to my soul,
And touch every sense with delight,
The magic is there in winter and spring,
In this city of music and light.

The pavement cafe a favourite haunt
For watching the world go by,
And seeing the legendary Danube flow
Reflecting the blue of the sky.

And everywhere is the music of Strauss,
From orchestras great and small,
Or even a street violinist playing,
Alone, by a palace wall.

The fiacres waiting in the street,
Are a glimpse of the days of yore,
But modernity also has its place,
So no one could ask for more.

Palaces, churches, concert halls,
Are beautiful to behold,
And here and there, on a roof or spire,
Is a glimmer of purest gold.

Magnificent ballrooms evoke the past,
In the music, the dance, the dress,
Chandeliers shine on the joyous throng,
'Tis a picture of true happiness.

Wherever I go in future years,
My heart will be here, it seems,
In this city of beauty, music and light,
- Vienna, the city of dreams.

Joan Letts

SPECTRES

Seated silently,
in a darkened room.
Enjoying the perpetual
entrancing, throbbing,
of the ancient timepiece.
The chimes struck twelve,
'twas then that they came.
Initially, the aroma,
a mustiness that crept
up my nostrils,
it tasted like death itself.
Then the emeralded glow.
An aura weaving
around the darkness,
encapsulating me
in dread and awe.
Then they followed,
like an infantry of warriors,
in neat procession.
Forgotten souls,
pained in life,
forgotten on interment
their wails,
touching my mortal soul.
Their mournful cries,
pleading for a release.
No words touched my arid lips.
For, just as they came,
surely they departed.
I was alone once more.

Claire Partridge

THE HARBOUR

The air is filled with seamen's cries
With clanking chains as anchors rise
Lapping waves against the quay
As fishing boats set out to sea
Sea birds circle in the sky
Wives and children shout goodbye

Small boats bob upon the waves
Shrouded in a misty haze
While further up among the reeds
A busy cormorant dives and feeds
The scent of sea salt fills the air
And otters play without a care

On the shore above the tide
Some seals are lying side by side
As they lie basking in the sun
Far off engines gently hum
Boats that left at early light
Are slowly sailing out of sight

Coiled ropes lie on the ground
Nets and floats are scattered round
A scene of quiet, gentle peace
Where dogs are resting at their ease
Till the boats come safely in
And the harbour's busy once again

Sarah Lightbody

My Country Lane

Oh country lane of my childhood days
How good to tread your path again,
To see familiar fields in the shimmering haze
Greened by the gentle summer rain.

Overhead the curlew swoops and trills,
My stream still welcomes me when trickling past,
Surrounded by my Yorkshire hills,
I know that I'm back home at last.

And on the verge my faithful seat,
Sits proud but battered by the years,
Like a sentry, waits in blistering heat
For the clouds to cool him with their tears.

So many hours I spent with you
Oh country lane of my childhood days,
You haven't changed, still the friend I knew,
I'll remember you always.

Elaine Beresford

MY RETREAT

There's a little whitewashed cottage on the cliffs above the sea
With roses round the doorway, and it's waiting there for me.
There are foxgloves in the garden, pinks and poppies, hollyhocks
And bashful little violets hiding underneath the rocks.

There's a seat beside the doorway that faces t'wards the sun
Where I can sit and meditate when all the chores are done.
With a faithful old retriever snoring gently at my feet
Dreaming dreams of youthful vigour, chasing rabbits in his sleep.

Inside this little cottage it's a pleasure to behold,
Chintz curtains at the windows, flower prints in green and gold.
Copper saucepans gleaming brightly ranged in order on the wall,
China teacups on the dresser, primrose border round them all.

There's music playing softly and a book beside a chair
Within an oak-beamed sitting room with flowers everywhere.
There's logs against the fireplace for when the evening's cool
And a tabby curled up in a ball upon a cushioned stool.

What more could one desire when one feels the need to flee
From the overwhelming pressures of this life's anxiety.
A little whitewashed haven on the cliffs above the sea
With roses round the doorway, and it's waiting there for me.

Patricia A Atkin

A Sad Farewell

Dear old house you stand forlorn
Your pride and beauty gone
Wind searches through the emptiness
Like the whispering of a song
From chimney stacks of crumbling stone
No wisps of smoke emerge
And rafters open to the skies
Now a refuge for wild birds
Chill air and dampness linger
Beneath the stained old stair
Where ants and beetles scurry
Below frail cobwebs hanging there
Fond memories of childhood dreams
Reach out with love and care
And pale ghosts seek the shadows
The bygone days to share
Through the bare and dusty rooms
Loving thoughts and silence roam
With aching heart and final glance
I bid farewell to home.

Rosamund Hudson

THE MONUMENT
(To Steph with love, Keith)

Standing on the Meridian Line -
Stepping over both sides of time.
The sky above begins to cry -
Wetting the grey green sea.
Looking out to the far horizon -
Watching the breakers rolling to the shore.
I think of you -
Encircles by your love -

And I am at Peacehaven with the world.

K D Thomas

SUMMER IN OKLAHOMA

The wind was warm, hot breaths from a
dusty land
clearing the heat-packed heaviness with
movement and life.
Almost-flat lands. Rolling into prairies,
thrusting wheat and sucking oil
and still red soil, cracked from the drought,
absorbing the sun.
Greens show pretty against the red,
leaves chewed and lacy,
trees welcome but fewer to the west,
grass wiry and fading.

Small towns with space between houses
but not between lives,
hugged close in common destiny,
the young still part of yesterday's generation,
nothing new but nothing old,
beginnings within memory,
mistakes erased with
no respect for history.

And everywhere churches.
Large congregations with activities
every night of the week,
every need of the member,
-social clubs and Sunday schools,
teaching and preaching and building and barbecues.

Air-conditioned automobiles large and dusty,
quarter-horses red like the sandstone rock,
and inside the houses cool and dim,
sharing and drinking iced tea together.

Jane Upchurch

THE OLD CHURCH

Entering the damp mustiness of the old church
My footsteps hesitated on the flagstone floor.
A silence surrounds me,
Except for the echo of the closing oak door.
A rectangular shaft of low evening sunlight
Cast a lone pale shadow across the narrow aisle
From a vast stained-glass window,
Rainbow coloured in faded medieval style.
The ceiling arched towards a magnificent dome
From whence a great myriad of mixed colours swept
Down to the cloisters below,
Meeting the stark lime-washed walls with dramatic effect.
High above the simple altar, a large cross hung
Dominating the chancel to the choir boy's stall
And precinct of the clergy,
A holy sign transcending in eternal recall.
The ancient lofty pews behind each other stand
In rows with ageing blackened hard uncushioned seats
And old initials sunk in grooves
Where children sit uneasily swinging dangling feet.

I sat alone in thought, beside a large stone pillar
Feeling an atmosphere of serenity and peace,
But questioning this wonder
This curious place where time seemed almost to cease.
A haven for pilgrims this great church must have been,
A monument for safety, shelter and prayer
A stately building steeped in history and care.

Isobel M Maclarnon

THE TRACK

No road came to the village,
Only the track, laid by countless,
Barefoot walking, five
Sole scorching miles to the railway,
Modern lifeline, in an ancient world.
And we, conditioned west, touching east,
First to negotiate, by car, and by darkness . . .
Thick, fog-like dust, swirling before
The headlights, too late, he saw
The fat, solid body writhe
Onto the track. We felt the bump.
Stopping momentarily, we looked back
From inside . . .
The snake had gone, disturbed, unharmed.
No sanitation came to the village.
We children never liked, going into the cotton fields
After dark . . .

Jacquie L Smith

A Winter Cold

Catch hold of the breeze
It only makes you sneeze
The winter cold
Makes one feel old
It weakens your strength
In every length
You struggle every morning
The outside is a yawning
The blizzards creep in
With this weather you can't win
A sheet of white blanket
Lays across your path
'Tis better you take a hot bath
Soak all your sorrows
And maybe tomorrow
Will be a better dawn

Suzan Gumush

THE ORCHARD

Strong golden arms
Bear red ruby globes
That lie, themselves around
The delicate emerald gems.

Row upon row they stretch
Far into the distance.
Shimmering in the half-light,
Sounding in the moonlight.

As their fruits are born,
Collection now is made.
Sold soon to all that want,
The globes are swallowed down.

Helen Lansdown

My Heavenly Garden

The garden for me is a close time with my God
His plants unfolding at my finger-tips
His flowers in my sight, in colours so bright
His earth so dark brings all feelings to mind
His seasons changing to relieve any boredom
His birds ever present, to sing a new song
His trees giving shelter and joy as I walk around
His sun, moon and rain the air that we breathe
His earth sea and sky all ensure me of His presence
                          if I am ever in need

Joan Marian Jones

IN HARPFORD WOODS

Where the giants stand, and caress the skies,
And their shadows mingle in dappled light,
I feel I am watched by a thousand eyes,
That will not allow me far from their sight,
Where the tangled bracken up to my knees,
Tries to hold me back, and restricts my tread,
A silence overcomes every tree,
And each bird ceases singing overhead,
This contagious silence soon overflows,
To smother even the sound from a stream,
And a stillness creeps over all that grows,
As if I were not welcome here, it seems,
Then from images where dark and light blend,
Come the flies, to greet me like some old friend.

Peter Chaney

UNTITLED

Before Christmas
The people
Not the nights
Definitely not the nights
Have drawn in
The houses have turned their backs
Lights have gone on
Curtains are not yet drawn
Between this cube of light
And that one
Is an interesting space
It seems to me
That you could plot
The mid-points of deepest dark
Between the lights
And following those
You'd have a footpath
Glimmered on at both edges
Only the sound of your steps
And the breeze
Rustling dry stems
To tell you where it has come from
And where you might go
A long way before dawn
That would be a lonely enough road
That no daylight
Could ever map

Malcolm Bell

THE EMPTY HOUSE

I pushed the oak door and entered,
The room felt dank and cold.
Cobwebs curtained the windows,
While thick dust covered the old
Black beams and the uneven floor,
As ash on the hearth from a fallen log,
Shivered and floated in the air,
Which came in through the open door.

I went quietly from room to room,
And quickly became aware,
That the house was not empty, but
peopled by men who had once lived there.
It was full of their whispers and shadows,
Their sorrows and happiness too,
The atmosphere of past families,
Once living and vital like you.

P R Mason

Lament For The Passing Of The Front Garden

Once upon a time, front gardens grew
Lawns and flower beds.
Occasionally, the odd small tree
Stood proud. Now instead
Of trim green turf there is pale concrete,
Smoothly neat tarmac,
Or handsome regulated paving -
'Guaranteed no weeds.'
Flowers no longer lift their heads to
Greet the morning sun.
Here, metal on rootless rubber lies
Abandoned to whim.
The rose expert has been replaced by
The car mechanic.
Caravans obscure the view from the
Old woman's window;
Closing in her boundary walls to
Imprison further.

Maureen A Jones

A Glen In Antrim

Your voice breathes
Perfume and fire
How you shine
In the clear Ulster dawn
The radiance of you
For you are all things
           To me.

Once you whispered
Telling me
Your secret name
And I trembled
Day turning
Into night.

My heart's desire
In the glens of Antrim
Aching
Longing
For your secret place

Julian Ronay

MEXICO

New land.
New country.
New people.
Warm glow,
On faces.
Smiling happy.
Looking out.
Helping out.
Caring warm,
Mixed people.
Red Indian.
Spanish people.
African people.
Poor happy,
Poor smiling.
New land.
New country.
Called Mexico.

Kiran Shah

IN THIS PLACE

No sound of music; no sound of birds' singing,
But silent stains of long-since suffering and pain,
   And still echoes of sticks on beaten buttocks bare
As men bent over, stretched on wooden bars,
While wet whips cut into flaking flesh to bone -
   Now only whining wind whips silent air.

No smell of spring: no smell of springing hope,
But a lingering sense of the stench of clinging death
   As men, worked out, worn out, were flung in trench,
And putrefaction filled the air in huts
Where guards did not dare to come and count or jeer -
   Now only threat of snow 'gainst barbed wire fence.

No sight of inmates; no more men in stripes,
But wandering travellers and stragglers, wide-eyed and sad.
   Across the flat, neat square where bleak winds blow
And grey gravel reflects a huge grey sky,
Beyond two huts - to show it as it was -
   Now pebble pits instead, stand row upon row.

No taste of wine; no warmth of Christmas coming,
But dry mouths, as of men on stakes, supports pulled away,
   Hung in death, as Christ on cross, though trapped
Not willingly - still, Jews, and other enemies of state
Killed by Nazis - 'By their fruit shall ye know them' - at this place
   Now deserted on a grey December day in Dachau.

Anne Byron

FLORENCE

To look across at Florence
Really broadens the mind
Set out in a valley
With mountains looming behind.

Red roofs on yellow houses
Take your breath away
Underlined by the blue river
Is more than words can say.

There are ancient bridges
As far as the eye can see
With shops over the river
Still the same as they used to be.

Paintings in abundance
Facing you everywhere
By the Great Masters
Are beyond compare.

Galleries with sculptures
Dignified and grand
As well as paintings
Of famous people of the land.

All nestled in between
Magnificent domes and towers
Bathed in Italian sunshine
As church bells peel out the hours.

Barbara Fosh

TY MAWR

Few strangers passed this way.
The Saxon Borrow or some vagabond
Seeing the friendly chimney
Might have crossed the gorse-lined brook
And begged a beaker of cold buttermilk
From the aproned busy dame
Whose husband tended sheep up on the hill,
On Sundays facing a far different flock
As he, black bearded, fierce, in mighty voice
Preached hell fire and redemption side by side.
They called him Jones Hell Fire, or, more polite,
Huw Jones Ty Mawr - Big House - no doubt
Because his farmhouse had four rooms.
His son, John Jones Ty Mawr, being less inclined
To athletic exhortation, three years running
Took the Bardic Chair and Crown.
While Evan, son of John, being curious
About those ills to which the flesh is heir
Packed little but the family name
And took a boat, and in due course
They made him Governor of Arkansas
Whence pilgrims come to seek - in vain -
The birthplace of this famous Celt.
At home a lesser relative moved in
But found the Ty Mawr legend hard to bear.
He took to drink and let the house burn down.

Two hundred years have passed. Once more
The people walk, but now from choice
And ancient paths restored bear honoured names.
That by Ty Mawr is now the Owain Glyndwr Way
And guides like Sid from Swansea show the way.
Sid, not erudite but helpful. 'No. Ty Mawr?

Can't say that I do.' And later
'Sorry, sir, no public toilets here.
But maybe if you was to go
Behind that heap of stones - 'And still
They have to cross the gorse-lined brook.

Bill Johnson

SPRINGTIME IN THE COUNTRY

It's seven thirty in the morning
In the countryside a new day is dawning
It lights up and becomes an amazing scene
Where everything is a wonderful colour of green.
Seeing the sunshine and the warmth it radiates
This is something I fully appreciate.

Hearing the birds whistle in the trees
Then watching them fly, they look so free.
Seeing all the animals roam
Looking as though they are at home.
It's the time of year the countryside thrives
When everything seems to come alive.

Looking up towards the sky
Lazily watching time go by.
Listening to all the different aspects of nature
Its sounds, are an outstanding feature.
Smelling the flowers in their full blossom
Springtime in the country is really awesome.

A cool breeze blows over its hills
All around feels peaceful and still.
Not having a worry in the world
For before your eyes, nature unfurls.
Springtime in the country tells its own story
It's great to be able to bask in its glory.

Hearing its rivers trickle slow
And seeing its clear waters gently flow.
Go to the countryside and sample its delights
For it is the most amazing sight.
Springtime in the country is a beautiful place
The freedom it gives, is so sweet to taste.

Neil McClafferty

IN THE MIDDLE OF THE NIGHT

Soft on the eyes, warming to the heart, comforting to reason,
seeming endless as time, soundless, it just seems to hover
From its vast expanse trillions of diamonds illuminate earth

Out of the still sky, rainbow water-drops cascade
Like silent bubbles they descend and transform into frozen flakes
Yet like fairy lights each one waltzes in the moonlit firmament
   dancing gracefully, somersaulting
     sublime they fall towards earth, twinkling like fireflies
soon they turn to ice, baby pearls, showering tears upon looming
buildings
   and the wings of shadowy skeletons cast ghostly figures

Towards city and countryside, the night hastens on, the white frost
lengthens
Its icy canopy creeps over the earth
At its calling, wells of water crystals stop
   when tenderly the freeze kisses the sparkling, soft flow
Casting its mantle over shining fountains and meandering streams
   it halts and almost stops the marrying flow,
     as it turns their surfaces into translucent,
     tranquil layers or cream

Encompassed with earth's fullness
   the world stirs, hope rises, despair is crushed
   the bitter and the sweet endure
Love and hate echo from breasted boxes
Alongside them dune citadels and mirrored edifices
   stand aflame, filled with wandering weary hearts
Yet elsewhere, other tireless watchers, contemplate
   hands raised, they look up and pray for the good of the nation

Levitating between heaven and earth, out of the thick black/blueness
   millions and billions of starlets, seesaw, suspended
   they gleam, shimmer and twinkle hovering above the world
   like dream-stones of restful hearts

Rosetta Stone

The Garden

A garden is a magic place where you can potter at a pace that suits you best and gives you time to see the flowers in their prime.

You wander through this fertile earth and realise a garden's worth is greater than a plot to grow the things you plant, the seeds you sow.

It gives you peace, it gives you space, a welcome break from life's rat-race, a quiet corner out of sight, a paradise of sheer delight.

It calms the nerves and soothes the breast, it give the tired brain a rest. The panacea of all our ills and healthier than any pills.

Feel stress disperse and tension fall and hope that it will make us all appreciate our garden more, now we know what it's really for.

Bob Wydell

The Cottage In Wales

Day will break, and dawn will take
The sheep down from the hill.
The sun comes up, and squirrels play
Beneath the window sill.
The river running downstream
Fresh brooks join here and there.
And if I ever loved you.
I think I loved you there.
A sun-kissed breeze moves from the trees
And dances on the river.
All is still but the daffodil
Bobbing her head with laughter.
The cottage below the mountain
Serene in the evening light.
Gives up her day and sleeps again
For the creatures of the night.

Sally M McNab

THE OAK TREE

So happy to be alive
my faithful friend called Horace,
he bounded off ahead of me
to our new discovered forest.

Quite dark it was beneath
the trees, the sky was almost hidden,
my trusted friend was not in sight
but would come if he were bidden.

So difficult it was to walk
with brambles in the way,
I wrapped my scarf around my face
on that cold December day.

So good the aroma of pine trees
and fern,
I was loving this walk
and would surely return.

Suddenly upon the hill
standing straight and bold,
with boughs outstretched a mighty oak
framed by a sky of gold.

I treasure so, that moment
I found my setting sun,
and caught a beauty infinite
that nature's hand had spun.

Olive Bedford

Pharmacy Warfare

As the waiting line grows longer, intolerance is a-brew,
Agitation bubbling, to get their say in too.
Clearing throats and angered sniffs, expressing they were first,
Stamping heels, adjusting weight, now growing aches feel worse.

In crowding packs, they congregate, to jam securely in,
Sharp the frowns of disrespect, no change of smile or grin.
Lacking English manner, they grumble in dismay,
Expecting instant service, as they ordered yesterday.

Solitary stand the chairs, for comfort while you wait,
To pushing hordes, 'tis ridicule, for fear they'd lose their place.
Elbowed in the rib-cage, shunted in the spine,
Cantankerously, they snarl, as hostile, throngs, entwine.

Sara Russell, Golden Eagles MCC

AS I SIT HERE (BELGIUM 1986)

As I sit here, where busy people hurry past.
And buttercups and tiny daisies pattern the new mown grass.
Where slowly, rivers glide and lazily sigh,
Between green banks and meadows sweeping gently down,
Neath an azure sky.

As I sit here, where white distempered walls,
Hide stonework, that whispers of distant centuries in time.
There the 'paddle-boet' plies its watery trade,
And tourists on their 'canal trips' gaze in wonder
As they glide beneath the ancient bridges
Here in Brugges.

As I sit here, the world races on, and cars and 'velos' hurtle swiftly by.
Past flower beds, hanging baskets overflowing
With mosaics of sweet smelling summer flowers
A source of joy to fill the eye with sweet delight,
The nostrils with heady, sweet perfume.
Nostalgia races back the years.
To other days.

As I sit here, gnarled fingers ply their craft.
Bobbins moved, undisturbed by the world's great throng,
On velvet cushions, made by generations long ago.
The sun strikes down, each small brass pinhead
Gleaming like a million sunbeams,
Caught in a web that human spiders weave.
The snow-like creation lies limp, its lacy perfection
Shown to its best advantage, cradled lovingly,
On the spinner's lap.

As I sit here, the ducks swim in flotilla,
Waving their tail flags and casting ribboned wakes
Against the twinkling ripples on the moving waters 'neath the weeping willow.
All is peaceful in this hypoactive city.
Even the ringed dove calls to make my mind's picture complete.

And I sit, and laze, in sweet contentment drinking in the golden sun.
For all is sheer delight, a peaceful rest
As I sit here, the landscape of ancient Brugges
At my feet.

Harry H Rolfe

Holiday Cottage

Little house nestled there
Built with love and so much care
Many feet have passed your door
Some to come some before

Warm and pretty there within
A place of peace away from sin
If you could talk of life and love
You'd tell each tale like larks above

A little place carved in stone
Amongst God's mountains is this home
Storm or tempest knocks your door
Where birds and beasts and eagle soar

Yet safe within your walls we feel
Away from hurt and life that's real

Susan Goldsmith

AS I LOOK UP

As I look up at the stars
Each and every night
They shine like diamonds
So lovely and bright.

A silvery moon glowing
In the midnight sky
Disturbed only as
A plane goes by.

The view is so
Peaceful and still
As I look up
From my windowsill.

It helps me to relax
After a very hard day
Preparing me for tomorrow
Whatever may come my way.

So the next time you
Are on the verge of a cry
Just open your curtains
And take a look up at the sky.

Ian Fowler

SUNDAY SCHOOL

Flowered bonnets on our heads
        Off we went when small,
            Along the passage and over High Bridge
Then by the grey church wall.

The big latch clicked as we stepped inside
        From the sun to the dim, damp chill,
            With stained-glass windows looking down
On that place so hushed and still,

We tiptoed to pews that were hard and cold
        To kneel and pray, or sing,
            Saw the curate glide by in his long black frock
And waited for bells to ring.

From the vestry door the vicar appeared
        With his wife (a fragile rose),
            A well-built man with greying hair -
And dewdrop on his nose!

Collecting our stamps we left the church
        Pleased to be out and free,
            Jumping the cracks as we skipped on home
In time for Sunday tea.

Maisie Cottingham

MEMORIES

I remember, I remember
The land where I was born
And the nostalgia I'm filled with
Makes me sometimes feel forlorn.

I remember, I remember
Golden beaches and the food
Balmy days, scented nights
Crickets and fire-flies in the wood

I remember, I remember
Tram rides through the city
The zoo, museums and cinemas
Beggars for whom I felt such pity

I remember, I remember
The bustling park where after school
My ayah used to take me to play
And watch dragonflies in the pool

I remember, I remember
The spotless convent where I went
The nuns were warm and wonderful
They were the happiest years I've spent.

I remember, I remember
The gigantic banyan tree in the park
Squirrels, snakes, various birds
Who sheltered 'neath it in the dark.

But although I remember
My carefree Indian childhood with a sigh
I'm in England now, it's home to me
This is the land where I want to die.

Margaret D'Sa

MY HAVEN

Haven of my heart you rest
among the islands of the west
'tis there the stillness of the night
melts gently into soft daylight

I see again the birch leaves
rustling silver in the breeze,
clear bird song hear to tease
the world to wakefulness.

The shepherd, collie at his heel,
strides swiftly on his upward way
to search for lambs who've strayed
and in the dark are lost and feel afraid.

Within my heart I hold remembrance
of our laughing youthful love.
The whole night long we'd dance
till morning called us from romance to
daily work.
When night released us from our toil,
we'd burn again the midnight oil.

I wish, just once again, I could be there,
to smell the clear sweet-scented mountain air,
to see that green and pleasant land at dawn of day,
and know I had come home to stay.

Christina Crowe

PORT ISAAC NORTH CORNWALL

Through the lamp lit cottage rows
The sea breeze lightly blows.
Wood smoke curls with the wind
From homely fires that burn within.
Here each road slopes to the pebbled shore
Where white foam-backed waves inward pour,
Fishing boats bob in its briny swell
On the edge of village light that pales,
Into the dark ocean's reach.
There the vast unseen waters break, hiss and breach
Across the craggy rocks of slate,
That hold the centuries of time and wait,
The unsuspecting roving eye to perceive
These charms this mild winter's eve.

Colin Farmer

INFORMATION

We hope you have enjoyed reading this book - and that you will continue to enjoy it in the coming years.

If you like reading and writing poetry drop us a line, or give us a call, and we'll send you a free information pack.

Write to :-
    Poetry Now Information
    1-2 Wainman Road
    Woodston
    Peterborough
    PE2 7BU
    (01733) 230746